Dearest Gilly!

My Dear friend.

We are

Simply Stunning
Beaded Jewelry

Translated from the Italian by Alyssa Barrett

Thanks to: Daniela, for her invaluable and attentive collaboration. Franco Boschetti, Carolina Malinverni, Emma Lombardi, Elena Villani, Isabel Nidasio

Library of Congress Cataloging-in-Publication Data available

10 9 8 7 6 5 4 3 2 1

Published in 2007 by Sterling Publishing Co., Inc.
387 Park Avenue South, New York, NY 10016
Copyright © 2003 RCD Libri S.p.A., Milan (Italy)
Published originally in Italian under the title *Gioielli con perline*
English translation copyright © 2007 by Sterling Publishing Co., Inc.

Distributed in Canada by Sterling Publishing
C/o Canadian Manda Group, 165 Dufferin Street
Toronto, Ontario, Canada M6K 3H6
Distributed in the United Kingdom by GMC Distribution Services
Castle Place, 166 High Street, Lewes, East Sussex, England BN7 1XU
Distributed in Australia by Capricorn Link (Australia) Pty. Ltd.
P.O. Box 704, Windsor, NSW 2756, Australia

Printed in China.
Sterling ISBN-13: 978-1-4027-3226-3
          ISBN-10: 1-4027-3226-0

For information about custom editions, special sales, premium and corporate purchases, please contact Sterling Special Sales Department at 800-805-5489 or specialsales@sterlingpub.com.

Simply Stunning
Beaded Jewelry

Donatella Ciotti

Sterling Publishing Co., Inc.
New York

Contents

Introduction

Jewelry has always been a status symbol, not only as an artistic expression that stirs up admiration and fascination, but more often as a means to show off power and wealth. For example, Henry VIII, King of England, had a 98-ounce gold chain that represented his regal power. The links of the chain were sold during periods of national financial crisis, because each piece corresponded in value with a monetary unit.

Throughout the centuries, people—particularly women—have used precious jewels to express their true personalities. Even the earliest known pieces of jewelry reflect our realization that there are an infinite number of ways to combine precious stones and valuable metals (not to mention inexpensive materials). They remain, to this day, true masterpieces.

Let's talk about the jewelry sold in moderately priced jewelry stores, perhaps most commonly known as costume jewelry—and we aren't alluding to the inexpensive "junk" that one finds in certain nonaccredited places, but rather to the creations that are generally put on display at fashionable stores.

Each precious material finds its doppelgänger, or pretender, in costume jewelry; for example, rhinestone and crystal imitate diamonds; plastic imitates amber resin; exquisitely cut glass beads suggest colorful, precious stones; and base metals, through special chemical baths, are dressed as gold.

The assembly techniques for costume jewelry and fine jewelry are identical: it's the human hand that gives life and character to art! It's enough just to know how to choose quality materials. From there, we can each explore our own paths in jewelry making, an art form that has been integral to our culture for years. The person who is always hungry for this art brings such a great passion to it that he finds himself instantly an artist!

With this manual, you can begin to establish your confidence in the basic techniques. We start with the necessary tools (covering everything from availability to utility, the different materials, and the rudimentary techniques of workmanship, and then we move to projects, giving you the simplest first and gradually increasing the complexity to designs you may have thought were impossible to make with your own two hands! The clarity and simplicity of the instructions and step-by-step illustrations will soon convince you otherwise.

Your jewelry box will be enriched with fantastically designed rings laid side by side with luminous earrings, sumptuous necklaces, stunning pendants, spiral necklaces of "one thousand and one nights," which you can pair with equally dazzling bracelets. The multilayered chokers will make you feel like you're living in the lap of luxury. Also, there are belts that will shine on your hips with classic, elegant simplicity; brilliant jeweled lariats that you can nonchalantly knot at your neck. Many more fantastic surprises await you on every page!

Multicolored American jewel in the form of a tree. The stones are mounted in an open setting, allowing the light to shine through the many-faceted crystals. The brooch is mounted on golden-colored metal.

Two-stranded necklace with Venetian pearls in varied shades of green.

This necklace is made of three strands of glass beads colored to imitate pearls. The pearls are interspersed with semiprecious stones. The decorative clasp, studded with rhinestones, gives evidence of the fine workmanship and costly price of the piece. In the height of fashion in the 1950s, this look, with its effect of light and grace, was particularly sought after.

History of beads

The story of glass beads unfurls across the streets of every country in the world and travels through the ages. The art of making glass beads, originally used as imitations of precious stones, developed primarily in the Ancient Egyptian period, then continued with the Romans, who created an infinite variety of blown-glass beads.

Roman beads, produced until 400 A.D. within the confines of the Empire (specifically in Alexandria, Antioch, and Rome itself), were highly admired for their exquisite craftsmanship and range of color, an art not to be matched until Venetian production began.

Along with Egypt and Rome, Islamic countries were also important centers for producing glass and, in particular, beads, which took on value as talismans. Together they developed new techniques that eventually led to the production of the famous "eye," "folded," "scallop," and "feather" beads.

After the fall of Damascus in 1401, bead production in the Islamic world encountered a decline (with the sporadic center of work in Asia Minor persisting). Venice became the most important center of glass and glass bead production, using practically every technique from centuries past in its production. On the Island of Murano, glassmakers concentrated completely on oven-work and baking. By decree from the Governor of the Republic, the production and distribution of beads were confined to the island so that the secrets of the work would not be revealed to the outside world.

Here on Murano, new methods of fabrication were born and developed (that of *paternostri,* literally Our Father, which imitated the grains of crystal used in rosaries, and *margarite,* which was created by cutting cane, to perle a lume and the famous *Conterie*). During the Renaissance people began to sew beads onto clothes, and some of the most seductive and fantastic elements of fashion began to appear.

From the end of the nineteenth century through the beginning of the twentieth century, the art of glass beadwork found fans in the teachers of Art Nouveau, like Emile Gallé, the great glassblower, and a few years following, the art was enriched by the production of

Tiffany; twentieth century jewelry triumphed with the refined women's clothing that was imposed by the fashion industry of the time. The commerce of beads wasn't as fully supported during the past century, and was generally reserved to particular sectors of employment. Recently, there has been a renewed interest in beading as a hobby, for individuals who want to try their hand at making something tailored to their exact taste. When supported by creativity and passion, these attempts often turn out to be artistic masterpieces.

This necklace of Venetian glass beads in different forms and dimensions exhibits classical artistic workmanship and extremely varied tones of green.

Wildlife is one of the preferred subjects of costume jewelry stores, but is less commonly found at a more upscale jeweler's. These pins date from 1970 to 1980 and are made with molded metal and a rhinestone spray, with both gold and brightly colored enamel parts.

Beads and crystals

Beads, those miniscule spheres of light and color, have returned during our time with the same triumph they enjoyed in other eras. Beads are used in woven clothing, for interior decorating, and, above all, for creative jewelry that flaunts all their magnificent possibilities. Paired with crystals, they are the protagonists of modern gem and jewelry design.

Of all the crystals found in renowned jewelry stores, Swarovski crystals are considered the most prestigious in the world. They were named for Daniel Swarovski, who, in a factory in Austria, invented a machine that could execute any given cut previously done only by hand. His invention greatly benefited the market. The cut and color of his crystals became famous. Especially noteworthy was a subtle and scintillating shade which, for its remarkable reflectivity, was called "Aurora Borealis."

The following examples illustrate the principal "champion" beads present in today's market.

Single bead – A bead of artistic workmanship in white filigree. Shown here is aventurine with a small ruby rose in relief, partially green and pastel, and set in a white filigree.

1 – *Multicolored glass*
Max Serale Stone (Tramonto)
Max Govinda Stone (yellow gold + aventurine)
Miró grass-green (yellow gold + tips of blue aventurine)
Worm-eaten grass (tarnished yellow-gold)
Evening-green fish
Evening-green rounds.

2 – *Swarovski crystals* in various forms.

3 – *French crystals* (little lanterns) and oval crystals.

1   2   3

4 — *Flowered beads*, the typical glass bead known around the world, with floral decoration. A central peak of aventurine, decorated predominantly with rose ringlets and small yellow and blue polka dots. The work on either side of these beads is very delicate and subtle.

5 — *Sandblasted mosaic beads*. These beads are made by first casting a base of pastel glass (a solid blue base), on which, by proper attachment, tiny decorated tiles are placed side by side. The whole bead is then set with heat and put in a bronze stencil.

6 — *Matte polka-dot beads*. Pastel glass beads with colored polka dots inserted, then quickly sandblasted.

7 — *Beads submerged in silver*, with a more brilliant color than the beads submerged in gold. The beads submerged in 925K had a center of colored glass, covered in silver leaf, and a "tarnished" dyed finish, either smooth or in relief.

8 — *Murano glass pendants*, made by hand with gold leaf. Delicate white lace.

4   5   6   7   8

How to thread beads

To create an aesthetically pleasing, valuable piece of jewelry that will last throughout the years, it's essential that you choose high-quality materials. It's inadvisable to use plastic beads—even though they are more affordable, they are poorly made and disappointing in their appearance. It's best to choose glass beads of equal size.

Before beginning, find a comfortable, well-lit place to work.

Next, lay a clean cloth or towel on a desk or tabletop, to keep the beads from rolling off the surface while you are working. Pour the beads into a large, relatively deep bowl. Cut a piece of string about 2 yards in length. Make a knot at one end. With the opposite end of the string, pick up the beads from the top of the pile and let them run along the length of thread. If you develop a steady, consistent rhythm, you will find that the beads practically thread themselves.

If you find a bead with a partially closed, blocked, or filled hole, open it with a pin or use a thinner thread that will fit through. Take a thread that is about 51", and tie off the end in a knot (the remaining thread will serve you in the following steps). Wrap the rest of the thread around itself into a ring.

Materials

Chain-nose pliers: to open small wire loops and close metal clasps.

Cotton thread: for beaded necklaces, bracelets

Crimp beads, crimp tubes, and end crimps: used to separate beads on a thread or wire or to close off a beaded thread or cord once you're finished.

Earring wires: for earrings.

Eye pins: used to join components, such as for earrings, when a small ring is desired at one or both ends.

Flexible stainless steel wire: a strong, flexible wire used in beading; made from multiple strands of very thin wire with an outer coating of nylon.

Flowered spacers: for decorative spacing between beads.

Glue: used to adhere crystals and beads to metal parts; also used to adhere threads together in a closing; cyanoacrylate is recommended.

Gold, silver, copper, and zinc wire: 20-, 22-, 24-, and 26-gauge; used for making rings, bracelets, and necklaces.

Head pins: used to close off necklaces, pins, and pendants; also used to join components.

Hypoallergenic materials: safer than regular metals for those with hypersensitive skin.

Lobster clasps: join two ends of bracelet or necklace.

Memory wire for necklaces, bracelets, and rings: a strong, sturdy wire used to make chokers and other shape-retaining jewelry pieces.

Metal cones: cap- or cone-shaped bead tips with premade holes; conceals beaded strands or threads.

Nylon thread: a single-fiber, elastic thread; sold in stores in various lengths, diameters, and colors.

Perforated disks, brooches, and clasps: beads are fastened by needle and thread to the holes in these findings.

Ring mandrel: measures circumference when bending wire into rings; provides a support for your work.

Round-nose pliers: used to give a round form to the wire, such as when shaping eyelets and small loops.

Ruler: for measuring wire, thread, and beads; should have both inch and metric increments.

Scissors: preferably with a sharp, angled blade.

Spacer bars: used in multistranded necklaces to maintain an even distance between threads.

Wire cutters: to cut metal wire neatly.

Wire threaders: of various lengths, depending on type of work and beads. Can be found for bead holes of various sizes; fitted to match elastic or nylon threads.

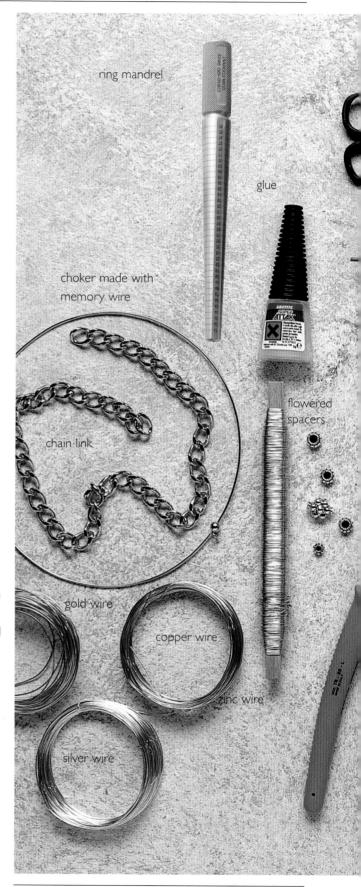

ring mandrel

glue

choker made with memory wire

chain-link

flowered spacers

gold wire

copper wire

zinc wire

silver wire

handmade beads

jewelry tag

flexible stainless steel wire

angled scissors

safety pins

NYLON COATED #48-7 LENGTH STAINLESS STEEL WIRE 100M

metal mesh

glasses holders

wire threaders

bracelet memory wire

T-shaped tool for wire wrapping

earring wire

earring wire

perforated clasp

metal flower bases

organza ribbon

earring wire

silicone thread

metal flowers

base for a broach

silver components

spacer beads

lobster clasps

base for a ring

head pins

seperator bars

crimp beads

flat-nose or chain-nose pliers

spacer beads

bases for rings and earrings

base for a pin

bead tips

decoration for an earring

round-nose pliers

wire cutters

perforated disk

Techniques

THREADING BEADS WITH KNOTS

1 – Pass the threaded needle through the clasp and make a small knot. Place a crimp bead around the knot and press firmly with chain-nose pliers to conceal the knot. Thread on a bead, press it firmly against the crimp bead, and make another knot to hold the bead secure. Continue to thread beads, separating them with knots on either side.

1

2 – Aside from simply looking nice, knots between the beads keep the beads from rubbing against one another and prevent the necklace from breaking or unthreading.

2

3 – To ensure that your knots sit firmly against the beads, push a pin or needle through the middle of each knot as you make it and pull tightly. Do this for each knot until the last bead is knotted into place. At the end, pass the thread through the end of the clasp and follow the directions in step 1 above for affixing the clasp and crimp bead.

The knotting technique illustrated here can be used to restore an old beaded necklace from your jewelry box or something you pick up at an antique jewelry boutique.

After you have repaired or replaced the broken beads, wash each bead in warm, soapy water, scrubbing off any residue, and rinse well. Dry the beads with a clean cloth. Never immerse beads in a solvent of any kind. Thread the beads, knotting them as you go, and affix a clasp of your choice.

3

WORKING WITH THREAD

1 – This technique is used when making rings, pendants, and bracelets. Thread several beads on a 10" strand of nylon thread. Bring the beads to the middle of the thread—the working area. Pass the two ends of the thread through the center of another bead from two directions.

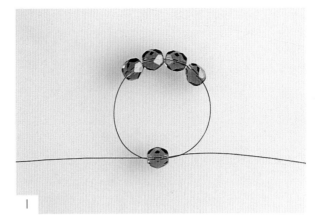

2 – Pull firmly on each end of the thread until the beads form a compact ring. Add more beads and tighten into a ring in the same way.

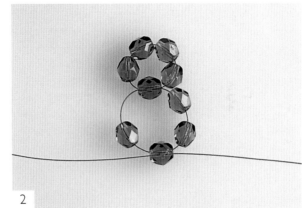

3 – To close off your work, tie the thread ends together in a knot; follow them with a bead and pass the thread through the center twice, gently pulling the thread so that it lays flat (both knots). Fuse closed with a drop of glue.

4 – For a variation of the technique, begin with two threads of equal length. Thread a single bead with both strands: one on the right, one on the left.

5 – Work both the right and the left strands, threading them alternately with beads, until you've reached the desired length.

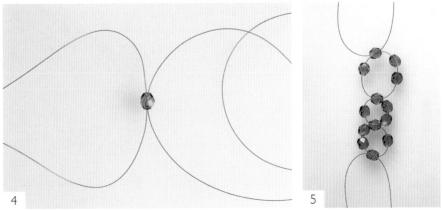

INTERWEAVING OR "LITTLE BOXES" TECHNIQUE

This technique is normally used to create bracelets, bags, and objects that need a basic, structured pattern. The example given here shows how to make a bracelet.

1 – Fold a length of nylon thread in half and crease slightly, forming a central point. Press a crimp bead around the point and pinch closed with pliers. This fastened knot is easily held in your hand and will make your work much easier. Thread 2 crystals on one strand and 1 crystal on the other strand.

2 – Cross one of the two strands through the center crystal and pull both strands tight.

3 – Continue inserting 2 crystals on one strand and 1 crystal on the other strand and interweaving the strands through the center crystal. Bit by bit, you'll see the pattern take form: tiny, interconnected flowers or boxes.

4 – To widen the work, interweave the next strand through a side crystal, rather than through the center. Insert 2 crystals on the outside strand and 1 crystal on the inside strand.

5 – Interweave the outside strand through the single crystal on the inside strand, to create a reverse curve.

6 – Interweave the inside strand through the next side crystal (counts as 1 crystal). Thread 2 crystals on the outside strand. Interweave the inside strand through the closer crystal on the outside strand. Continue this pattern of successive loops to join the new pattern to the existing work.

7 – To finish, pinch a crimp bead firmly around both strands.

8 – Pass each remaining strand through the crystals to an end of the bracelet. Form a small loop and attach a clasp.

TYPES OF CLOSURES

1 – To seal a **closure with a crimp bead**, thread on all the necessary beads, ending with a metal crimp bead. Insert the end of the thread back into the crimp bead and through the last bead on the strand, forming a loop at the open end. Firmly pinch the crimp bead closed with flat-nose or chain-nose pliers.

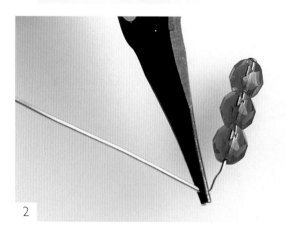

2 – For a **loop closure**, thread the beads on a head pin or eye pin; push the beads all the way to one end. With flat-nose pliers, gently bend the end of the pin about 1/4" from the closest bead. Cut the wire at this point.

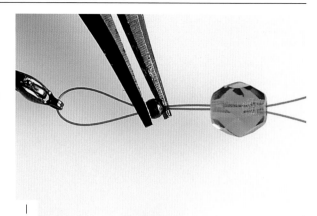

3 – With round-nose pliers, slowly wrap the wire end back on itself, forming a small ring.

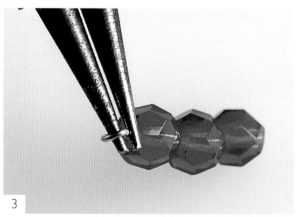

4 – For a **hook clip closure** (the most common closure in commercial markets), pass the end of the beaded strand through the hole in the hook clip. Thread a crimp bead onto the strand.

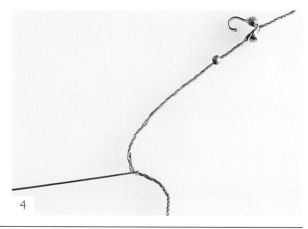

5 – Pass the crimp bead along the strand until it rests snugly against the hook clip. With flat-nose or chain-nose pliers, squeeze the crimp bead tight around the strand until neither half of the bead moves. Cut off the excess thread. Using pliers, close the hook clip, concealing the crimp bead and any loose thread ends.

6 – For a **jump ring closure**, grasp the ends of the ring with round-nose pliers and slowly open outward in opposite directions, going as far as possible without deforming the ring. You should never bend the ring out too far because it will lose its "elasticity" and won't fully or securely return to a closed position.

7 – When you need a **2-thread closure**, for example, at the end of a necklace or bracelet, thread both strands through the hole of a hook clip and make two very tight knots.

8 – Cut off the excess thread and put a drop of glue on the knot. Use flat-nose or chain-nose pliers to push the sides of the clip together, concealing the knot.

9 – For **cord closures**, insert the end of the cord in a crimp end and pinch closed with pliers until secure. The cord should not budge, even when pulled.

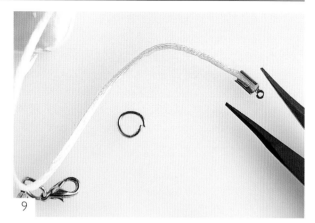

FASTENING HANGING JEWELRY AND PENDANTS

Use this method for lariat necklaces, which present decorations at the end and close with a knot, rather than a clasp.

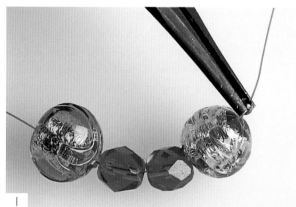

1 – Place the pendant or hanging pieces at one end of the thread (nylon or nylon-coated stainless steel wire, depending on the kind of beads you're using). Insert a crimp bead at one end and pinch it closed firmly with pliers.

2 – Position a crimp bead at the base of the last bead and close it firmly with pliers (if the beads are heavy, you might place crimp beads between each bead). Continue adding the beads until you're pleased with the appearance. Close off the end of the necklace in the same manner as you began. Remember that you can insert more than one strand of thread into a single crimp bead.

USING HEAD PINS AND EYE PINS

1 – Thread the beads on the head pin. Trim off the excess wire 3/8" to 1/4" from the last bead. Use round-nose pliers to bend the wire end into a small, open ring. Thread and close off an eye pin in the same way.

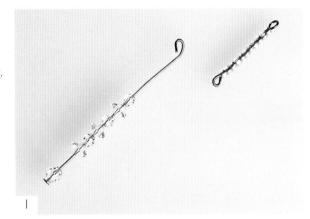

2 – To join two pins, place an open ring inside a closed ring. Close the ring firmly with flat-nose or chain-nose pliers to lock the pieces together.

3 – You can connect various pieces in any order you wish.

4 – Here is an example of a pair of earrings made with pins. They are suitable for daywear or evening and are easily made in many different variations to satisfy your every whim!

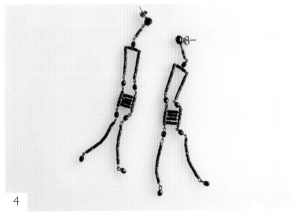

FIXED KNOT

1 – This knot is best made when using thick thread, such as the rattail shown here. Knot both ends of a single length of thread. Wind one end of the thread once around the other end, making a loop. Hold all the threads firmly, but keep the looped end of the thread free.

2 – Wind the free end around the core threads a few times to secure them: these loops serve to enlarge the knot and make it stronger. During this process, avoid crossing the coils—try to keep them in order, one beside the next. Crossing the coils will add volume to your knot, but the knot will come undone more easily, and you want to avoid this.

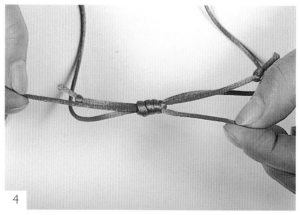

3 – To close the knot, pass the free end of the thread through the part of the loop that extends beyond the coils.

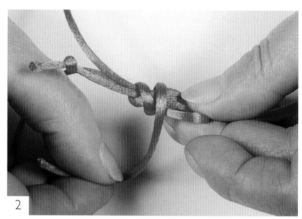

4 – Carefully pull the two ends simultaneously. The knots at the ends will prevent the thread from sliding through as the knot tightens. This method is easy and quick, and the knot is small and discreet. In addition to being useful, it can serve as an extra decoration or stylistic element, particularly when making ethnic-style necklaces.

LOCKED LOOP

1 – Fold a group of strands in half to form a loop. Wrap one of the threads once around the base of the loop. Draw the end of the thread through the loop just made and pull snug to make a scalloped knot.

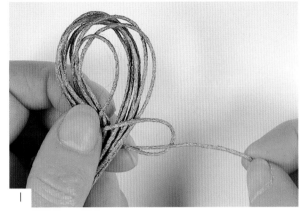

2 – With the same free thread, make a scalloped knot around the strands of the large loop. Pull the thread firmly to secure the knot.

3 – Continue making scalloped knots, paying particular attention to keeping the profile of the knots uniform and compact.

4 – After you've finished the entire loop, wrap the thread around the base of the loop and make a scalloped knot. Repeat once or twice until the work is secure.

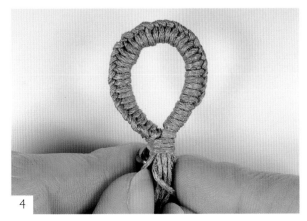

Projects

Mother-of-pearl waterfall

Materials
- 3 strands of violet water pearls
- 1 strand of white pearls
- 1 strand of tube-shaped pearls or opalescent beads
- 7 assorted pieces of mother-of-pearl
- 3 1/4 yards beading wire or thread
- fasteners or crimp beads
- wire cutters
- flat-nose or chain-nose pliers

This necklace is made with three separate lengths of pearls, joined with pieces of mother-of-pearl.

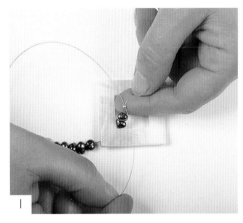

1 – Cut a 14" length of beading wire. Thread on several beads and pearls in any order you wish. Add a crimp bead at the end. Slip the strand of beads and pearls through a piece of mother-of-pearl. Pass the longer end of the strand through the crimp bead to form a loop.

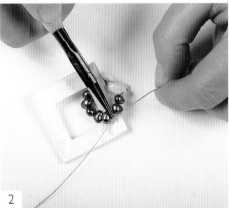

2 – Draw the loop closed, so that the bead section forms a ring around the mother-of-pearl. With the pliers, pinch the crimp bead to seal the ring. You have now made the first part of the necklace.

Repeat two more times until you have created 3 separate pieces. Thread beads and pearls on the long wire ends. Link the three beaded strands together into a single ring by looping the ends through the mother-of-pearl pieces and crimping until secure. Add three more beaded strands, so that there is a double strand between each mother-of-pearl piece.

3 – To make the mother-of-pearl waterfall, cut a 5" to 7" length of wire. Make a loop around a fourth piece of mother-of-pearl using the method described above. Add beads to the longer wire end and loop it through one of the mother-of-pearl pieces on the necklace.

4 – With the pliers, pinch a crimp bead to close off the loop. Cut off the excess wire. Continue until you have made 3 or 4 strands of your mother-of-pearl waterfall.

Carnelian cascade necklace

Materials
- 1 large ring of carnelian
- 14 smaller rings of carnelian (various sizes)
- 4 or 5 packets of small cylindrical beads
- 2 bead tips
- 4" chain link
- nylon thread
- 2 head pins
- lobster clasp
- wire cutters
- transparent glue
- roud-nose pliers

1 – To make the centerpiece, join the large carnelian ring to a smaller ring with a small string of beads; close the beaded ring with a double knot.

2 – Join another small carnelian ring to the large carnelian ring, making a slightly larger ring of beads to connect them. Close off the beaded ring with a double knot. Continue joining small carnelian rings to the large carnelian ring or to each other to form a loose triangle for the centerpiece of your necklace. Reinforce your rings by placing a dab of glue on each knot you've made.

3 – For the necklace, thread 10 strands of beads, each measuring 16". Divide them into two groups of five strands each. Fold each group in half to find the midpoint. Affix the midpoint of one group to one side of the carnelian centerpiece, using two beaded rings (instead of one, as above). The two rings will help support the necklace and also add to the design. Follow the same directions to join the second group of beaded strands to the other side. To close off the necklace, bring the strands on each side together, making sure they are equal in length so the necklace will hang properly. Before cutting the thread, seal the ends of each strand with transparent glue to bind them together. On each side, push a head pin through the strands and wrap it around itself. Place the bead tip over the end.

4 – With pliers, close off each end and gently pull out the pin. Cut the pin to about 3/8". On one end of your necklace, using round-nose pliers, attach the lobster clasp, bending the nail into a small ring. On the other end, affix the piece of chain link (or bend the pin into a loop). The advantage of a chain is that it allows adjustments to the necklace length.

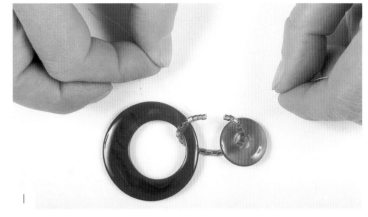

1

2

3

4

Evening jewelry

Materials
- 15 black metal
  beads
- 415 black crystals,
  Ø 6 mm *
- 166 black crystals,
  Ø 4 mm
- 32 black crystals,
  Ø 8 mm *
- 1 packet of black
  beads
- about 40 eye pins
- flexible steel wire
  in black, 28-gauge
- jump ring
- lobster clasp
- chain link
- flat-nose or
  chain-nose pliers
- round-nose pliers

*Ø= mathematical
   symbol for diameter

1 – Using the interweaving or "little boxes" technique (page 18), make 10 wheels of 10 small squares each; use 6 mm black crystals for the outside and middle positions and 4 mm beads for the inside position to form a graceful curve. To close off each wheel, pass the outside strand through the first crystal. Knot the strands and cut off the excess. Make one slightly larger wheel for the center of the necklace using 8 mm and 6 mm black crystals.

2 – Using a new wire, join two wheels; they will make up one side end of the necklace. Insert a wire through one of the outer crystals of a wheel. Thread 2 crystals onto one side and 1 crystal onto the other side. Insert the wire with 2 crystals into an outer crystal of a second wheel. Knot the strands to draw the ring closed and cut off the excess.

3 – To give this choker necklace its shape, join a third wheel in the same way, except substitute small beads for the crystals. (This third wheel will become the second wheel on the top row of the necklace.)

4 – Continue joining the wheels, using a combination of small beads and 5 crystals between the wheels, until 7 wheels are joined together, forming the top row of the necklace. Make sure the larger wheel is in the center. Complete the second side end piece in the same way you created the first.

5 – For the center oval (which bears a flower in the middle), make a strand of 21 small squares. Join both ends to the center wheel of the top row of the necklace. Using the same method, make two other ovals and join them to the second wheel in from each end of the top row of the necklace.

6 – Insert a strand through a black metal bead and attach it to the base of the center oval. Do this with four other beads. Then, on one of two strands, insert a crystal to create the center of the flower, thread the strand through in reverse and twist all the strands together at the base. Insert 2 new strands through the center bead of the flower. You now have 4 sections of thread that you'll fill with beads and attach to the center oval. Join the remaining 2 wheels to the lower part of the necklace, between the ovals. Using the black metal beads, make two more flowers. Join them on either side of the center oval, between the upper and lower wheels.

On one end of the necklace, connect a chain link, and on the other, a lobster clasp.

7 – For the fringe, insert a crystal on an eye pin and cut off the excess. Form the end into a small ring with the help of round-nose pliers. Join the pieces together and close the rings.

8 – Continue to make and join the crystal pieces until you've completed the lower part of the necklace with a gentle cascade.

5

6

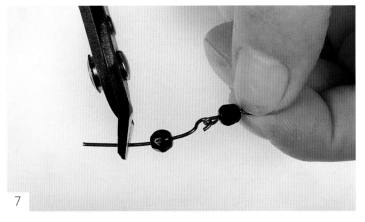

7

8

Jeweled "scarves"

Materials
- 182 black glass
  beads of various
  shapes
- 7 1/8 yards waxed
  string
- 5 3/4 yards of
  braided silk thread
- 6 5/8 yards black
  minicord
- 26 cord ends
- 70 eye pins
- flat-nose or chain-
  nose pliers
- round-nose pliers

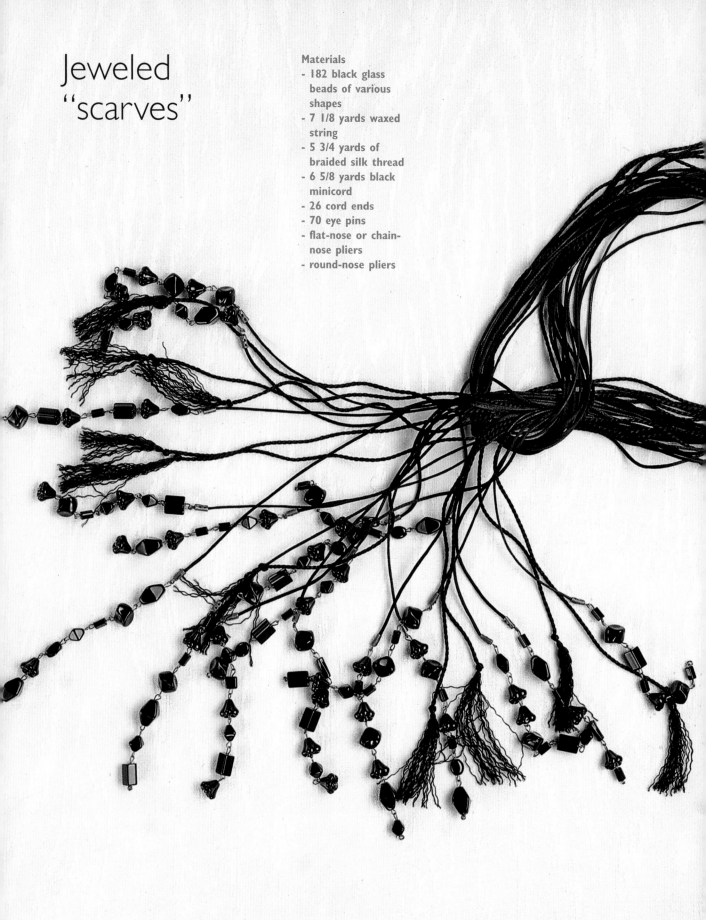

1 – Cut the waxed string into five 51" pieces, the braided silk thread into four 51" pieces, and the mini-cord into four 59" pieces. Insert a cord end on each end of every 51" cord; use the flat-nose pliers to pinch the sides closed.

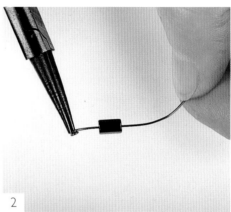

2 – To begin the fringe, insert a glass bead on an eye pin. Close off the base by making a small curve in the pin with the round-nose pliers.

3 – This prepared bead has a loop at each end..

4 – Using the method described above, join the bead components to create individual strands of the fringe, each using 7 glass beads. Insert the

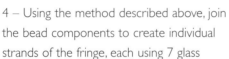

final pin of each fringe in the cord end you prepared earlier, and close it off by making a small ring. Prepare all the other cords in the same way, bunch them together, and tie one central knot to bind them. Fasten the scarf around your neck with a loose slipknot.

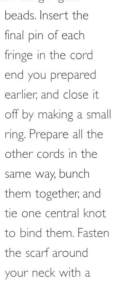

On the left— Variation of the scarf in white with cascaded pearls.

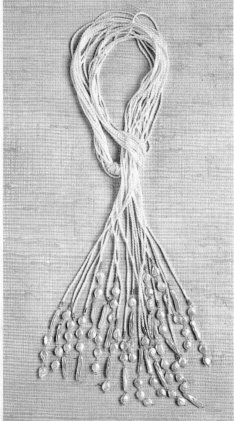

Two-faced Swarovski pendants

Materials
- **for each pendant,
  180 Swarovski
  crystals, Ø 4 mm**
- **nylon thread**

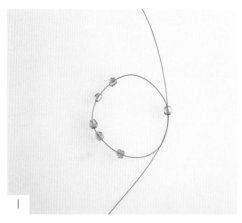

1

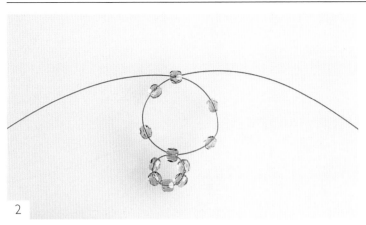

1 – Cut 60" of nylon thread. Thread on 6 crystals and center them on the thread. Cross the two ends of the strand through the middle of the last crystal you threaded.

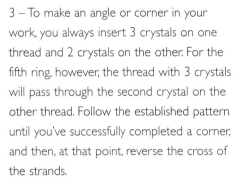

2 – Insert 3 crystals on one of the threads and 2 crystals on another. Insert the thread with 2 crystals through the third crystal on the other thread, and pull tightly. Continue in this way until you've formed 4 crystal rings.

2

3 – To make an angle or corner in your work, you always insert 3 crystals on one thread and 2 crystals on the other. For the fifth ring, however, the thread with 3 crystals will pass through the second crystal on the other thread. Follow the established pattern until you've successfully completed a corner, and then, at that point, reverse the cross of the strands.

3

4 – For the second (inner) layer, push one of the two strands through the two crystals from the first layer and then add another crystal on the thread; on the other strand, thread 2 crystals and cross this strand with the single crystal (which you added) on the other strand. To make the corner, pass the strand below the fourth crystal on the first layer and, in exiting, insert another crystal; cross with the other strand.

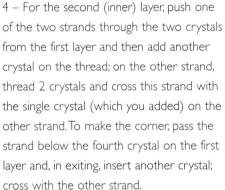

4

5 – To make the second face of the pendant, cut a new piece of string and pass it through 3 crystals above the top interior corner of the first face. Insert 2 crystals on one end of the thread and 1 crystal on the other: cross the thread with 2 crystals through the single crystal.

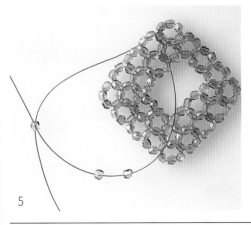

Follow these directions until you've completed the second part. Secure each strand well.

5

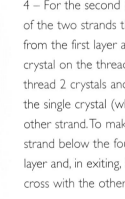

Pendant
chokers

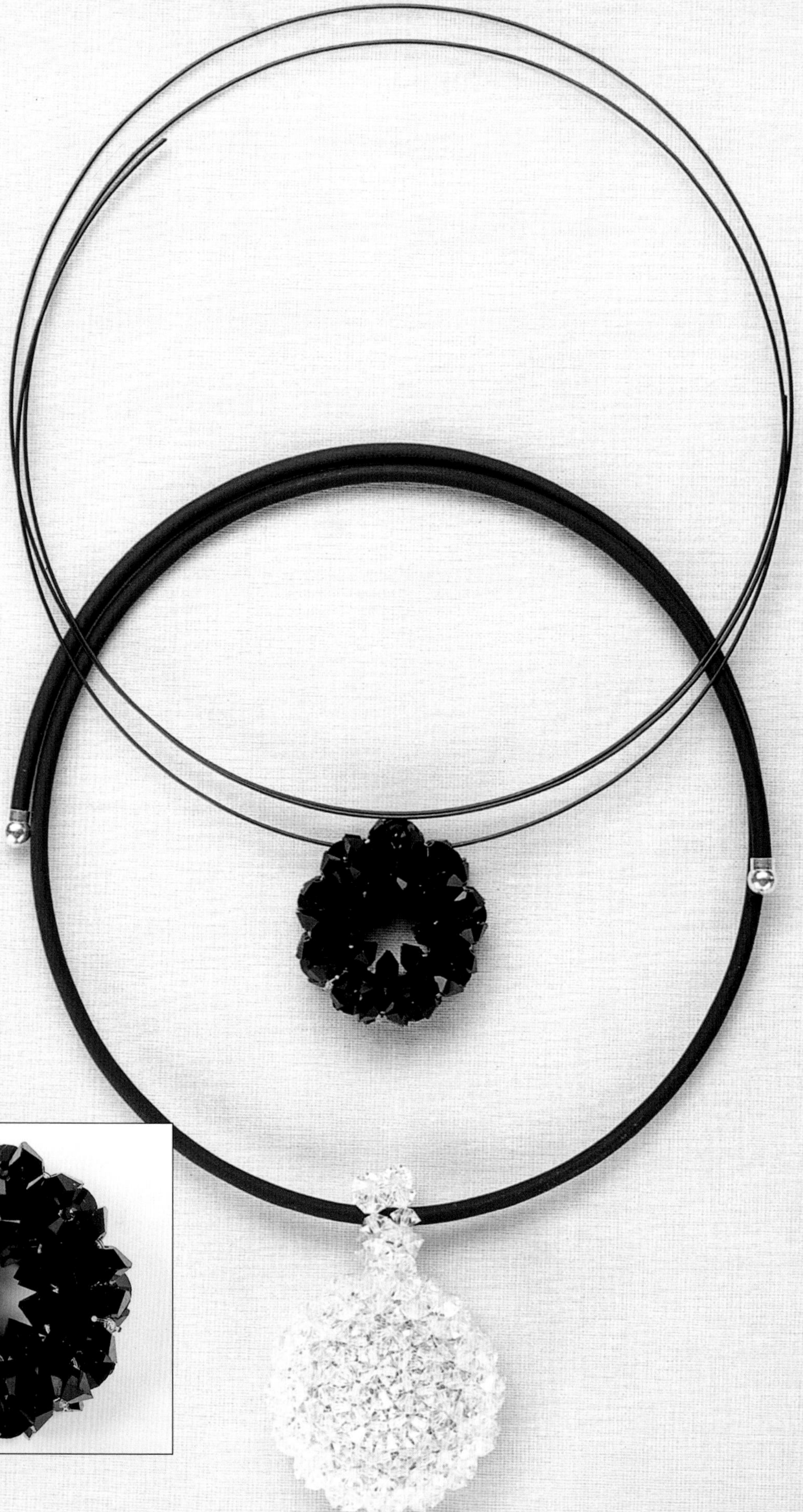

Materials
- 81 black angled
  Swarovski crystals,
  Ø 6 mm
- nylon thread

1 – Cut a 32" length of thread and insert it through 5 crystals. Cross the strands through the last crystal, bringing your work to the center of the strand.

2 – Insert the left strand through 1 crystal and the right strand through 3 crystals. Cross the strand with a single crystal through the last crystal on the other thread. Take care never to flip or turn your work; keep everything flat. Following these same steps, continue until you've made 8 joined flowers.

3 – To make the ninth flower, which is the closure, insert the left strand through 2 crystals and the right strand through 1 crystal. Use the strand with 2 crystals to pick up the side crystal of the first flower made. At this point, tie both strands together with a double knot (see technique on page 17). Make a second wheel, identical to the first, which you will stick to the back of the first in order to give form and support to the pendant.

4 – To join the two wheels, cut a 32" strand of thread and pass it through 2 adjacent crystals of the same flower. Thread on 1 new crystal and then pick up 2 adjacent crystals on the other wheel. Continue in this pattern until you have completely joined the 2 faces. Finish with a double knot.

Necklace with
embellished center

Materials
- about 50 glass flowers
- 10 packets of glass beads in various shades and colors
- 1 perforated clasp with 5 strand holes per side
- 10 gold-capped bead tips
- 10 head pins, gold
- nylon thread
- flat-nose or chain-nose pliers
- round-nose pliers
- transparent glue

1 – With nylon thread, prepare 60 strands of beads in various shades and colors, leaving 16" of empty thread on each side so that you'll have plenty to use when making a knot.

Group the strands in 5 bundles of 12 strands each. For each bundle, knot the strands and insert a head pin just below the knot. Do this at each end.

2 – Seal each knot with glue. With the round-nose pliers, shape one end of the pin into a small ring around the knot.

3 – Place a bead tip over the pin, concealing the knot.

4 – Insert the protruding end of the pin through a ring on the back edge of the clasp; cut off the excess wire. With the round-nose pliers, bend the pin into a small ring until secure. Repeat these steps to attach all of the remaining bunches to the clasp. Attach the opposite end of each strand to the other side of the clasp.

5 – To create a pattern on the perforated disk, insert nylon thread in the center hole. Block off the thread that pokes through the underside with a crimp bead, and then push the thread back through to the front. String on beads and flowers.

5

6 – Jumping over the last bead threaded, run the thread back through the beads on the strand in reverse. Bring the strand through to the underside and crimp. Bring it to the front and string on more beads and flowers. Continue in this way to create a pattern of your liking.

On the preceding pages – Variation on the necklace and centerpiece using beads and pearls.

6

Necklace with circles

Materials
- 4 packets of beads, Ø 6 mm
- 3 packets of beads, Ø 4 mm
- nylon thread
- chain link
- lobster clasp
- flat-nose or chain-nose pliers

1 – Using the interweaving or "little boxes" technique (page 18) and 4 mm beads, make a long strip that is 12 squares long and 3 squares wide. Beginning at one end, make a seam that joins both sides of the work to make a tube: Insert another piece of thread through 2 outside beads—one on the right and one on the left; run one of the strands through a new bead and then, through that same bead, cross the second strand. Pick up another bead from each side edge and continue the seam until the end of the work.

2 – Bring the ends of the tube together and insert a single bead on both strands. Now, with one of the two strands, pick up the bead at the front end. Make a double knot to close off your work.

3 – Pass one of two strands through the bottom bead, closest to the knot, and through the adjacent bead, in reverse; with the other strand pass through the other adjacent bead. Thread a bead on one of the two strands and cross the threads. In this way you have created a lateral small square.

4 – Pass the two strands through the center beads and on the end of one of the two strands, insert a bead. Cross the strands and make a double knot. Hide the threads inside the beads and cut off the excess.

5 – To make connector pieces, use the same "little boxes" technique and small beads.

5

6 – Complete each connector piece in the desired length: shorter for connecting the rings, longer for the sides of the necklace. At the respective ends of the necklace, attach the chain link and the lobster clasp to close.

6

Lariat necklaces

Materials
- 426 crystals or
  beads, Ø 4 mm
- 6 packets of
  turquoise-colored
  glass beads
- crimp beads
- nylon thread
- flat-nose or
  chain-nose pliers

1 – Using the interweaving or "little boxes" technique (page 18) and the crystals, make 1 wheel and 1 square (see the previous projects, pages 35 and 49, for directions).

2 – Prepare 3 strands of beads 32" in length and 4 strands of beads 51" in length. Loop the 32" strands through the crystal wheel.

3 – Run the same bunch of strands through the crystal square. Close off each strand with a double knot. To secure the strands, wrap 2 circles of 9 beads each around them close to the crystal square.

4 – Do the same on the bunch of strands looped around the crystal wheel.

5 – On each end of a 51" strand, thread on a crimp bead and squeeze it closed with pliers.

6 – For even more security, add 2 beads to each end, add a crimp bead, and squeeze it closed.

7 – Loop the 51" strand through the middle of the crystal square and tie in a loose overhand knot. Join the remaining strands in the same way. Run the strands through the crystal wheel to close off the necklace.

8 – For the turquoise necklace with crystal and beaded fringe (below), prepare the 51" strands with small beads, large beads, and crystals of your choice, finishing off each strand with crimp beads.

Below – Variation with cascades of turquoise beads in two sizes, intermixed with miniature crystals.

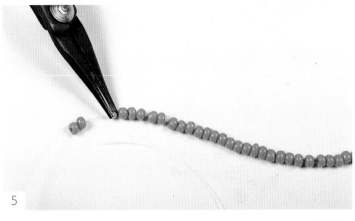

5

6

7

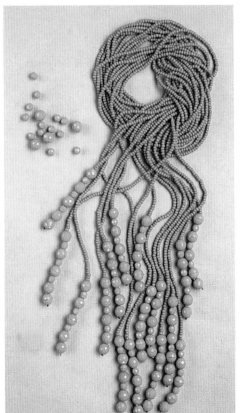

8

Embellished
mother-of-pearl

Materials
- mother-of-pearl disk
- stones and beads of your choice
- thin silver tubing
- 1 clasp (see step 6)
- 2 strand spacers
- nylon thread
- glue
- crimp beads
- wire cutters
- flat-nose or chain-nose pliers

1 – Glue 2 strand spacers to the back of the mother-of-pearl disk. Allow to dry completely.

2 – Begin to apply the stones around the mother-of-pearl disk with nylon thread: Secure the nylon thread at the back of the mother-of-pearl piece with a crimp bead. Run the thread through a hole on the edge to the front of the disk and add a bead. Pass the thread through the preceding hole and exit through the back of the disk (the seam on the back).

3 – Continue these steps until you've covered the circumference of the flower engraved on the disk (note that photographs 3, 4, and 5 do not show the complete beading). When you reach the starting point, knot the thread ends together and seal with glue. You now have a base on which to build the eyelet-rings.

4 – To fill in the edge with eyelet-rings, attach a new strand and close off the back with a crimp bead. Add 5 stones and make an eyelet by entering and exiting the holes. Continue until you have covered the entire edge of the disk. Secure each thread with double knots, run the ends back through various holes and beads, and, finally, cut off the excess. You have now created a small crown around the mother-of-pearl disk.

5 – To make the necklace, thread stones on a nylon thread for about 7". Run the thread through the top holes of the strand spacer, covering the space in between with glass beads to hide the thread; follow on the other side with 7" of stones. Thread stones and beads until all holes in the strand spacers are used, gradually increasing length of each thread to give the necklace its curve. More than one thread can go through one hole of the strand spacer.

6 – On each strand end, insert crimp bead and 3/8" of silver tubing. Pass strand through the first clasp eyehole, draw it up, and pass through again.

7 – With pliers, pull the strand firmly but gently so the silver tubing forms a snug loop around the eyehole; pinch firmly with pliers to close. Cut off the excess with wire cutters. Repeat until all strands are joined.

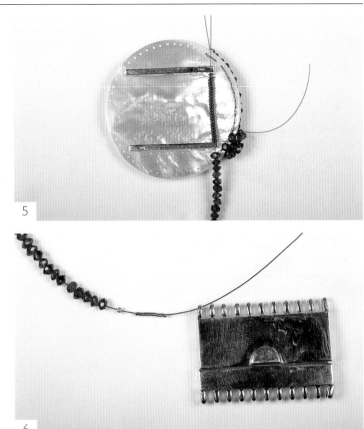

5

6

7

Jewelry with unpolished stones

Materials
- natural stones with silver supports
- pearls, mother-of-pearl, Biwa pearls, rose- and violet-colored pearls
- narrow silver tubing
- electrical wire
- flat-nose or chain-nose pliers
- chain link
- spring clip

On the opposite page—
Close-up of a necklace
made with strands of
citrine quartz and a
black agate stone in the
center.

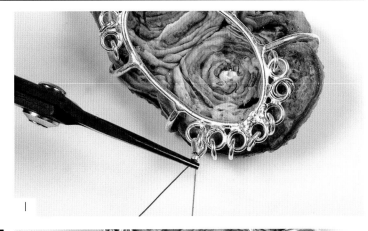

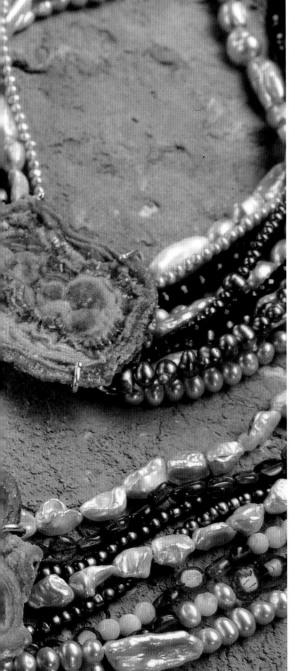

1 – Affix the wire to the silver support using a crimp bead and a
3/8" piece of silver tubing.

2 – Bring the wire back up through the crimp bead, making a loop
on one side to close.

3 – Fill the wire strand with the pearls of your choice to create a
pleasing array of shapes and colors. Continue until you've covered
all the holes in the silver support. For the closing, group all the
strands together at one end, closing them off with crimp beads.
Attach the chain and spring clip in the usual way.

Gem crosses

Materials
- 31 crystals (20 yellow and 11 black)
- gold wire, 24-gauge
- organza ribbon, 24"
- flat-nose or chain-nose pliers

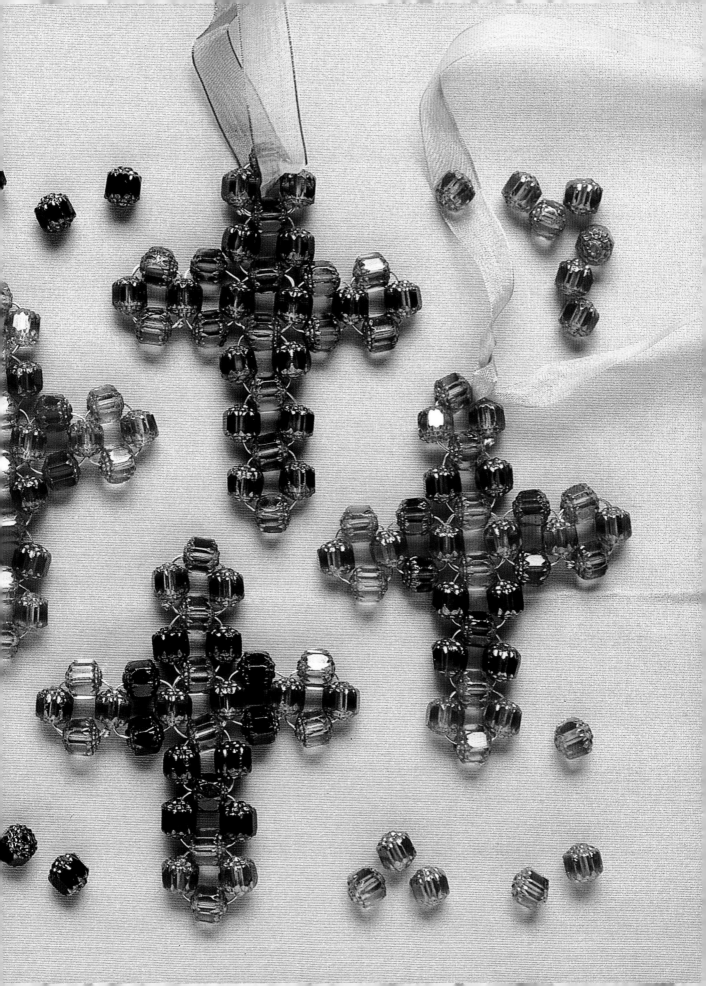

1 – Thread 4 crystals on the wire, bring them to the center, and cross the ends of the wire through the bottom crystal. Add 2 crystals to the left side and 1 crystal to the right side (compare your work with the photo on the right). Cross the right thread with the left thread in the center crystal at the bottom of your work. Repeat this step 6 times, referring to the chart (opposite page, bottom right) for the color scheme.

2 – At the end of the last step, after you have crossed the two wires, pass one wire through the last crystal again, pull the strands together, and twist securely with the flat-nose or chain-nose pliers. Cut off the excess and hide the ends inside the crystals.

3 – For the arms of the cross, thread 4 crystals on a new wire, as in step 1. Add 1 crystal only on each side. Cross the wires through a side crystal in the vertical section completed in step 2. You have now made the first arm. Pass the wires through the center crystals and cross them through the side crystal on the opposite side to begin the second arm of the cross.

3

4 – Add 2 crystals to the top wire and 1 crystal to the bottom wire. Cross the bottom wire through the middle crystal and pull snug. Repeat the process to add three more crystals. Pull to adjust and secure the structure and shape. Finish using the same method as in step 2. You have now completed the cross.

4

The finished cross, and the pattern to follow when creating it.

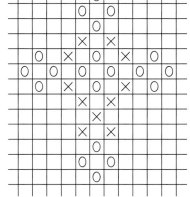

O   yellow
X   black

More crosses

Materials

Bordeaux cross
- 9 Bordeaux crystals, Ø 10 mm
- 18 small antique gold caps
- 1 centerpiece of your choice
- metal wire, 22-gauge
- round-nose pliers

Big black cross
- 44 crystals, Ø 6 mm
- 13 rhinestone roundels
- metal wire, 22-gauge
- round-nose pliers

BORDEAUX CROSS

1 –Cut about 8" of 22-gauge wire. Make a small hook at one end with the round-nose pliers.

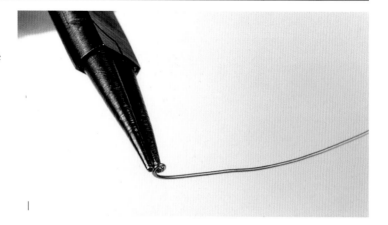

2 – Thread the components in the following order: 1 gold cap, 1 crystal, 2 caps (facing in opposite directions), 1 crystal, 1 cap, and centerpiece. After the centerpiece, thread on the same components in reverse order so that the two sides mirror one another.

3 – After you've added the last gold cap, make a small hook in the wire, as you did at the beginning, to close off the work. This completes the horizontal arm of the cross. With a new length of wire, repeat the process described above to make and join the vertical part of the cross.

BIG BLACK CROSS

1 – Cut a 12" piece of 22-gauge wire. Thread on 6 crystals and close off into a ring, leaving about 2" of empty thread on the end. On the longer wire, thread 1 crystal. Join the wire to the opposite side, forming a center for the ring, like a flower.

2 – Continue by threading on a roundel and making a new flower with 6 crystals. Follow the same steps to make a third flower.

2

3 – At both ends of the flower strand, thread on 1 roundel, 1 crystal, 1 roundel, and 1 crystal. With the round-nose pliers, make a small hook at each end. You have made the horizontal arm of the cross.

3

4 – With a new length of wire, repeat the method described above to complete the lower vertical arm of the cross, composed of two flowers. Insert a roundel as you affix it to the horizontal arm.

5 – To secure the wire, wrap it around the base of the roundel. With a new wire, make and connect the upper arm of the cross (one flower) in the same way.

4

5

67

Necklace with burned pearls

Materials
- 10 packets of burned pearls
- 4 packets of seed beads in brown-gold
- 6 packets of round, shiny pearls in brown
- 2 separator bars, 20 holes each
- 8" chain link
- 2 lobster clasps
- crimp beads
- iron wire, 26-gauge
- round-nose pliers
- electrical wire, approximately 26-gauge, enough for the desired length of your necklace
- jump rings

1 – On a separator bar, affix electrical wire with a crimp bead, and fill the wire with burned pearls. With the same technique, affix the end of the wire to the other separator bar. Continue in this way, filling each strand with the pearls and seed beads in any order or arrangement you wish until you've used all the holes on the separator bars. The strands should measure about 18" when filled.

2 – With the round-nose pliers, gently open two jump rings and attach them to either end of the separator bars. Insert a lobster clasp on each jump ring, then, using pliers, gently reclose the rings.

3 – Divide the chain link into two parts. Attach both pieces to the second separator bar, aligning them with the lobster clasps on the first bar.

4 – If you want, you can embellish your necklace with small flowers made with square beads or round beads. Make 5 double-ringed petals and close them off by attaching the wires at the base of the petals, from which you will later hang them.

5 – Use the hanging strand to make the center of the flower. Bring it through the back to the front of the flower, thread it through a burned pearl, then bring it back through in reverse and secure it to the other wires. Make 5 flowers in this same way.

6 – On the back of each flower, bend the hanging wires into small loops and attach them to the strands of pearls in the necklace. Cut off any excess wire.
To accompany the necklace, you can make a matching bracelet (see photograph on pages 68–69) using the same technique described for the necklace. Earrings can be fashioned on a ready-to-use, perforated, hypoallergenic base.

Sophisticated chokers

Materials
Black choker
- 5 packets of black beads
- fur flower
- metal jewelry wire, 24-gauge
- base support for fur flower
- organza ribbon

Turquoise choker
- 5 packets of turquoise-colored beads
- glass leaves
- crystals in various sizes
- jewelry wire, 24-gauge
- lobster clasp
- chain link

1- String the beads on a 6 1/4-yard length of wire. Wrap the strand into a skein, forming 9 loops, each 25" long. Fold the skein in half, to make 18 strands.

2 – Wind another strand of beads around the strands of the skein, making a few very tight loops to fasten them. Do this at both ends.

3 – Pull the excess wire away from the base of the secured loops and cut it.

4 – At the midsection of the choker, weave a piece of metal wire through the strands of the necklace, 2 strands at a time, to form a supporting "seam."

5 – Conceal the wire "seam" by weaving in another wire threaded with beads. You have now nearly finished the choker, which is open in the back.

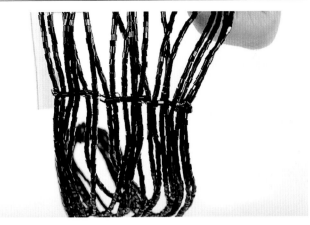

5

6 – At one open end, attach the chain link, and on the other, attach the spring ring or lobster clasp. Finally, apply the fur flower, affixing the back of it to the "seam" with small, hidden stitches. Tie on lengths of organza ribbon to close the choker.

6

7 – For the turquoise choker, follow the directions above for the black choker, but substitute an attractive composition of glass flowers and beads for the fur flower. If you like, you can apply fringe instead. Close with a lobster clasp and chain.

7

Simple necklaces

Materials
- 15 3/8 yards of silk-wrapped metal thread
  in various shades of pink
- 2 bead caps
- glazed glass cylinders or beads in various
  shapes and sizes
- 1 piece of thin metal wire
- 2 head pins
- spring clip
- chain link
- flat-nose or chain-nose pliers

1 – Cut the silk-covered metal wire into 35 pieces, each about 15" in length. Thread various glazed glass cylinders or beads on a number of pieces of the wire. Do this to your liking.

1

2 – Group all the strands together so that the ends are level and equal in length. Bind the ends together with a piece of the thin metal wire. Do this at both ends.

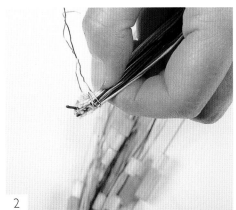

2

3 – Insert a head pin into each bound end of silk-covered strands and secure with the remaining metal wire.

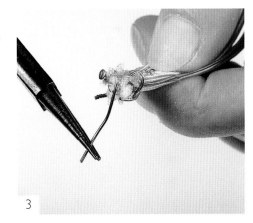

3

4 – Place a bead cap over the end of the head pin (which should stick out) and squeeze firmly with flat-nose or chain-nose pliers until closed. Follow the same step on the other end. Cut off the excess head pin, and shape the remaining wire into a small ring. Attach the spring clip to the ring. Do the same on the other side, but attach the chain link to the ring.

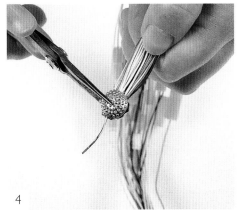

4

Multiwire necklace

Materials
- 2 lengths of memory wire (necklace-size)
- 3 separator bars with 20 holes each
- 3 mother-of-pearl flowers
- 5 packets of turquoise-colored glass beads
- cat's-eyes of your choice
- 3 supports for the flowers
- jewelry wire, 22-gauge
- eye pins
- Velcro hook-and-loop fastener
- glue
- round-nose pliers
- flat-nose or chain-nose pliers

1 – Cut the 2 lengths of memory wire into 15 equal rounds. Cut down each separator bar to 15 holes (instead of 20).

2 – Insert memory wire through a hole on the separator bar and slide bar to wire center. Thread beads on the wire to left and right of the bar, stopping about 3/4" from ends. Slip a separator bar onto each wire end. Continue threading beads until you've reached each end. Secure last bead on each end with drop of glue. Repeat until every memory wire is threaded with beads and joined to separator bars.

3 – At center of each flower, insert 2 strands of metal wire. Thread a cat's-eye onto each strand; use a small loop to close off wire.

4 – Use metal wire to secure a support to the back of each flower; do not cut the excess wire now. Thread 2 beads onto an eye pin. Attach pin to support edge by making a small loop in the wire. Repeat. Add beads, in pairs, to eye pins and connect loops together to create a fringe.

5 – Attach flowers to the choker with metal wire you didn't cut. Apply Velcro tape to back of choker, where ends overlap, so Velcro is hidden (attach Velcro to inside of one end and outside of the other).

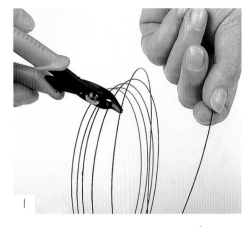

1

2

3

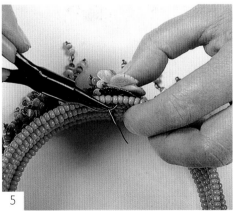

5

4

Wire and wire

Materials
- T-shaped tools, small and large, for wire wrapping
- metal wire in the desired color
- metal or silver wire, 28-, 26-, and 24-gauge
- hoops (to fit on earring hooks)
- earring hooks
- memory wire choker
- beads and crystals
- round-nose pliers

1 – Insert the metal wire through the hole of the small T-shaped tool and pull it through. Gently fold over a piece at the end so that the wire won't slip out.

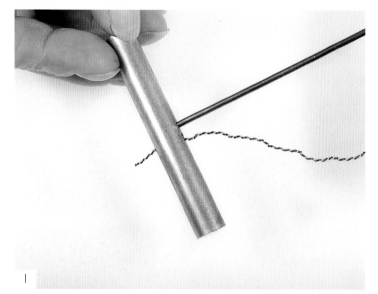

1

2 – Hold the T-shaped tool still with one hand. With your other hand, wrap the wire around the entire length of the T-shaped tool (about 6"), paying attention not to overlap the wire.

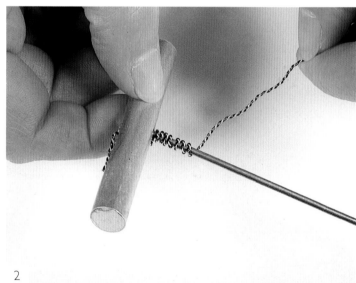

2

3 – Cut off the excess wire at each end of the 6" spiral. Carefully remove the spiral from the T-shaped tool.

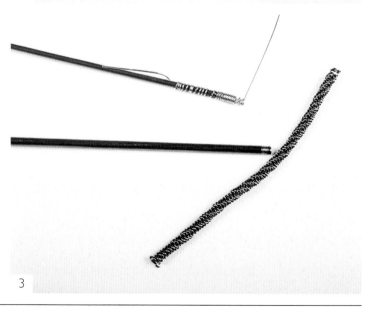

3

4 – To make a double spiral, thread 24-gauge metal wire through a 6" spiral and attach the end of the wire to the larger T-shaped tool. Wrap just the wire a few times around the T-shaped tool.

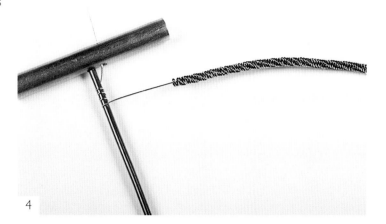

4

5 – Continue by twisting the whole spiral (with the wire inside it) around the T-shaped tool. Finish by wrapping the plain wire around the T-shaped tool a few more times to firmly secure the work. Cut off the excess on each end, and pull the double spiral off the T-shaped tool. Thread the wire pieces on the choker interspersed with beads or crystals.

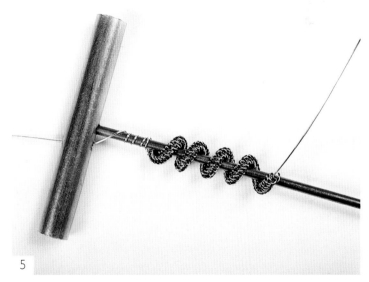

5

SPIRAL EARRINGS
1 – Make a double spiral with 5 layers. Cut off the excess wire on each end and pull the spiral off the T-shaped tool. Firmly close off one end with pliers, but leave the other end open until you complete the second earring. Then close off both earrings, making them exactly the same length.

1

2 – Open the small ring at the base of the earring hook, being careful not to deform it. Attach the ring to the closed end of the spiral you've just finished.

3 – With round-nose pliers, reclose the ring, squeezing it firmly between the small spirals.

HOOPS

1- To make large hoop earrings, unhook the ring of the hoop and thread on, in order: 2 beads, 1 three-layered spiral, and 2 beads. Reclose the ring by hooking it back into itself. Lastly, connect the earring hook to the hoop.

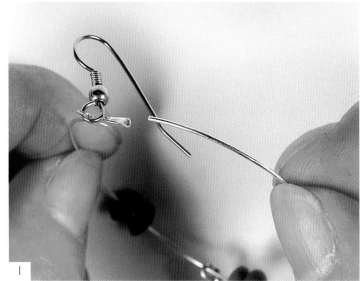

2 – Here is how the finished hoops will appear. You can choose any decorations and elements you like, to match your earrings to your wardrobe.

CHOKER

1 – Thread various glass beads on a 26-gauge metal wire and make a spiral using the large T-shaped tool. Cut the excess wire on either end and pull the spiral off the T-shaped tool. Insert a 24-gauge metal wire through the spiral and make a double spiral (as explained on page 83).

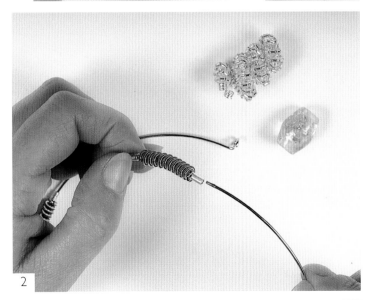

2 – Use a 28-gauge wire and the smaller T-shaped tool to make a very thin spiral. Thread a 26-gauge wire through the small spiral and make a double spiral with 10 layers. Make each turn using only the wire, and cut off the excess on each end. Make another double spiral identical to the one you've just finished. On the steel memory wire, thread on, in order: 1 double spiral, 1 crystal, the beaded spiral, 1 crystal, and 1 double spiral.

Spring necklaces

Materials
- 1 rigid memory wire choker
- 2 packets of ruby-colored seed beads
- 1 packet of jet-black beads
- metal wire, 24-gauge
- black silk
- vinyl glue
- wire cutters
- round-nose pliers

1 – This project is made using the "pole" technique. Cut a 6" piece of 24-gauge wire to serve as the "pole." Thread 3/4" of ruby seed beads onto the pole and slide them to the center. Place another wire at the base of the beaded section and twist to attach it. Thread some beads on the new wire, enough for the first inside curve of the petal.

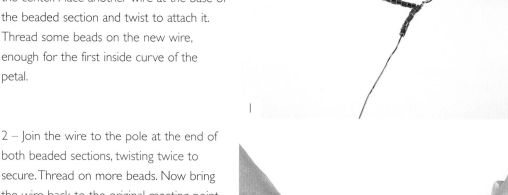

2 – Join the wire to the pole at the end of both beaded sections, twisting twice to secure. Thread on more beads. Now bring the wire back to the original meeting point of the two strands and twist twice around the pole to secure. Continue in this way, adding a relatively equal number of beads on the left and right sides on each round, to build the petal out from the center pole.

3 –Make as many turns, or passes, around the pole in the above manner, as you need to obtain a petal of desired size. To close off the strand, bring the wire up through the back and wrap it around itself, making a final pass; cut off any excess. Make 5 petals for each flower.

4 – With the black beads, make a strand. Make a small petal using the pole technique. Then twist the wire up to form a sphere, and squeeze it tightly to form a small ball for the pistil. Don't cut the wire—you'll use it when making the flower.

5 – Assemble the flower by uniting the various petals to the pistil, which is placed in the center. Tie the base together securely using a separate strand of plain wire.

5

6 – Thread some black beads on wire, bend into a loop, and twist the wire around itself at the base to close it off. This is the first small leaf of the branch.

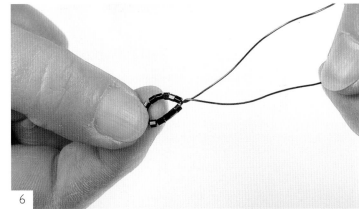

6

7 – Continue constructing the branch—without cutting the wire—by making new leaves in a nicely composed arrangement.

7

8 – Make as many different branches as you want. Join them together tightly with the black silk thread, using a bit of glue. Make leaves and flowers and, always using silk thread, tie them to the center of the rigid memory wire choker. Bring the strands through to the back, fasten them, and cut off the excess.

8

Choker with Swarovski flowers

Materials
- 172 double-cone Swarovski crystals, Ø 4 mm, for each flower
- large crystal for the center of each flower
- memory wire choker, covered in black silk
- nylon thread
- pin base
- earring base
- flat-nose or chain-nose pliers
- glue

1 – Cut 59" of nylon thread, and thread on 4 crystals. Bring the crystals to the center of the strand and cross the strand through the last crystal. Put 1 crystal on the left strand and 2 on the right. Cross the left strand through the last crystal on the right strand. Continue until you've made 6 small squares using this method.

1

2 – To close off the small squares, add 1 crystal on either side and cross each strand through the last crystal on the opposite side.

2

3 – After you have crossed the strands, bring them around in reverse, through the first side crystal.

3

4 – Add 3 crystals on the left strand, and 1 on the right, and cross the strands through the last crystal.

4

5 – With one of the two strands, pick up the bottommost crystal of the small square. Thread 2 crystals on that same strand, and 1 crystal on the other, and cross the strands through the single crystal. Continue until you've made the sixth small square.

5

6 – To close off this wheel, thread through the bottom and side crystals, inserting 1 crystal on each strand and crossing above one of two crystals.

6

7 – Work until you've made two full turns in the method described above; at the end make a classic knot. Seal with glue. You've made the first petal. Make 7 petals total.

7

8 – Once you have the completed flower, affix the center crystal by inserting a piece of wire through the crystals. The pendant is now ready to be attached to the necklace. If you wish to make a pin, insert the remaining wire through the holes in the pin base, securing it against itself with a knot and cutting off the excess.
For earrings, use the same technique.

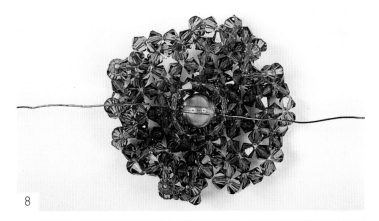

8

Flowered chokers

Materials
- memory wire choker, covered in black silk
- turquoise-colored crystals in various sizes
- leaves, feathers, and various glass elements
- metal jewelry wire, 24-gauge
- glue

1 – Thread various components on the wire.

2 – Shape the wire into loops with 5 crystals and 1 novelty bead each; let the novelty bead dangle from the bottom. Twist the wires together to secure the loops

3 – Create more loops in the same way, for a branching effect.
Proceed as described above until you have made multiple branches.

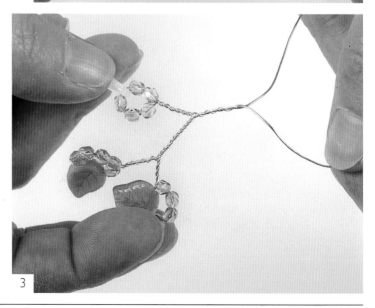

4 – Wind the black silk around the branches first, and then attach it to the base of the collar, continuing to wrap with silk.

5 – To secure the silk wrapping, add a drop of glue every so often.

6 – After you have covered all the branches, use a bit more glue to secure the base, and cut off the excess wire.

Flowers for the décolleté

Materials
- 10 metal flower bases
- 10 metal roses
- 50 Swarovski crystals, Ø 5 mm
- 1 packet of seed beads
- metal wire, 28-gauge
- small jump rings
- lobster clasp
- 20" of chain link
- earring hooks
- glue
- round-nose pliers

1 — Cut a 20" length of wire and insert it through a petal at the base of a metal flower, leaving a small tail in the back. On the front part of the wire, thread on a crystal and bring the wire back through in reverse.

1

2 — Bring the wire back up through the hole at the base of the crystal, and thread on a few small beads until you've covered the length of one side of the crystal. Bring the wire back through.

2

3 — Return the wire to the front and follow the same steps on the other side of the crystal to completely surround it. Continue in this way until all the petals are decorated and the entire face of the metal flower base is covered.

3

4 — Twist the remaining wire at the back and cut off the excess. Glue a metal rose to the center. Once you have completed all the flowers, join 8 flowers with jump rings, which should be closed firmly with round-nose pliers. Join the remaining two flowers with lengths of chain link. Attach the lobster clasp.

To make the coordinating earrings, affix the earring hook to the outer end of a petal of the finished flower.

4

Victorian choker

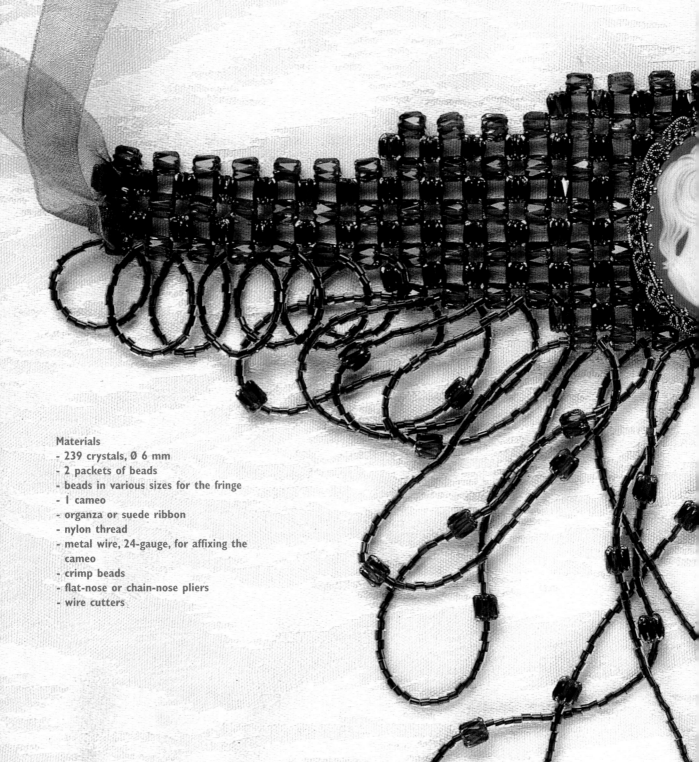

Materials
- 239 crystals, Ø 6 mm
- 2 packets of beads
- beads in various sizes for the fringe
- 1 cameo
- organza or suede ribbon
- nylon thread
- metal wire, 24-gauge, for affixing the cameo
- crimp beads
- flat-nose or chain-nose pliers
- wire cutters

1 – Using the interweaving or "little boxes" technique (page 18), make a rectangle that is 7 × 6 crystals in dimension for the center of the choker. Finish by tying the threads together in a double knot.

2 – On each shorter edge of the central block, add 9 crystals to make 4 little boxes along the edge.

Proceed with the same technique until you have completed one square, 4 × 4 beads in dimension, on each side. Then add one rectangle, 7 × 2 beads in dimension, at each end. Always close your work with a double knot.

3 – To make the fringe, thread a nylon strand through the center crystal on the lower edge of the center block. Thread on beads and crystals for the desired length, and then bring the strand up and cross it through the same crystal where you began. Repeat these steps on the next crystal. Continue in this way, making a succession of loops and always running the strand back through the starting crystal, until you reach the end. Then return to the middle and work out to the other end.

4 – Close off each end of the nylon thread using a crimp bead.

5 – Position the cameo in the middle of the center block. Pass metal wire through the predrilled edge of the cameo and bring it through to the back of the block. Twist the wire together securely and cut off any excess.

5

6 – On either side, tie organza or suede ribbon between the crystals.

6

Return to the Victorian style with this exquisite choker in jet black and with a snow-white cameo centerpiece. Tie it around your neck with black suede or organza ribbon.

Crystals and mink

Materials

For the belt (page 107)
- 372 crystals, Ø 6 mm
- 90 crystals, Ø 4 mm
- 1 packet of seed beads
- 5 mink pom-poms
- long pieces of mink or leather
- nylon thread
- dyed sewing thread
- hand sewing needle

For the necklace
- 144 crystals, Ø 8 mm
- 2 packets of seed beads
- 5 mink pom-poms
- long pieces of mink or leather
- nylon thread
- dyed sewing thread
- hand sewing needle

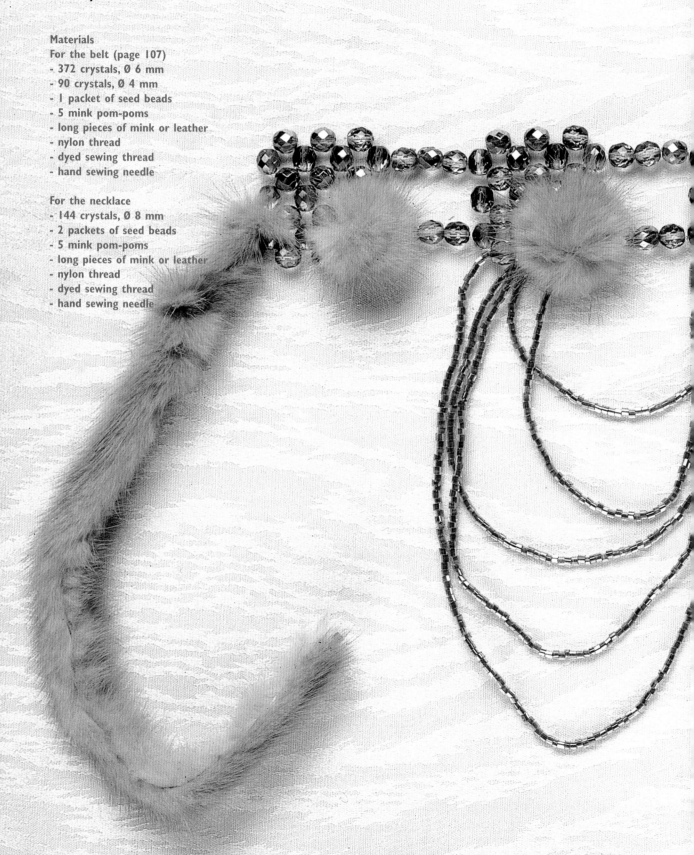

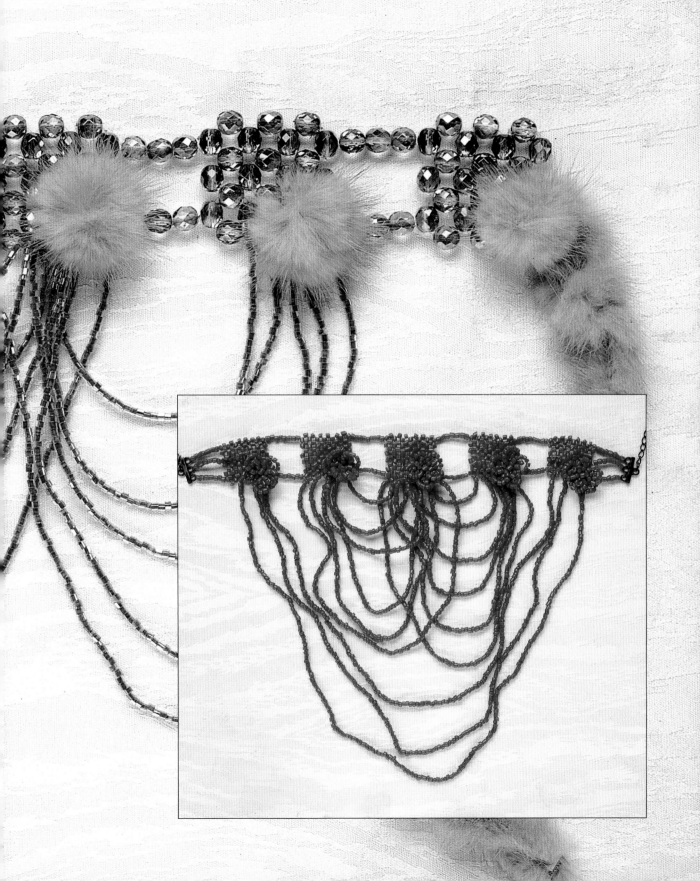

1 – To make the belt: Using the interweaving or "little boxes" technique (page 18) and the 6 mm crystals, make 2 squares, each 5 × 5 crystals in dimension, and 2 rectangles, each 5 × 11 crystals in dimension.

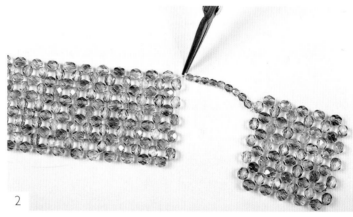

2 – To join the squares and rectangles, thread 10 crystals (Ø 4 mm) onto a nylon thread, connect the end to a beaded square, and secure with a crimp bead. Thread the other end to the corresponding crystal on a beaded rectangle and close with a crimp bead. Repeat 2 times, for a three-strand join. Join each of the components in the same way in the desired order.

3 – Sew a pom-pom at the base of each component with needle and thread, until firmly attached.

4 – At each end of the belt, slip the end of a long piece of mink or leather between the squares, fold it over onto itself, and secure with small, hidden stitches. If you are using leather, you can sew pieces of fur on either end for decoration.

5 – Use the same technique to make a necklace that matches the belt. To make the fringe embellishment, thread strands of seed beads and attach them to the lower edge of the crystals with crimp beads. Form graceful arcs of various sizes to create a shimmering cascade or waterfall effect. This type of fringe can also be applied to the belt to make it more precious.

5

Laced-bead
necklace

Materials
- **6 packets of assorted glass amber beads**
- **2 strands of semiprecious stones, about 32" each**
- **2 bead covers**
- **nylon thread**
- **2 head pins**
- **lobster clasp**
- **4" of chain link**
- **crimp beads**
- **flat-nose, chain-nose, or round-nose pliers**

At right — Variations of the same necklace design using different materials.

1 – Fill 16" of a 24" nylon thread with glass amber beads. Repeat until you have 34 strands, in various tones.

Bend a head pin into a ring. Insert a crimp bead on one end of a loose strand (but don't close it). Pass the end of the strand through the ring and back through the crimp bead. Now pinch the crimp bead closed, forming a small loop to affix and secure the strand to the head pin ring. Repeat for each strand, and then repeat at the other end. It would be too time-consuming, given the number of strands, to tie a knot in each piece of thread.

1

2 – At either end, insert a head pin. Place a bead cover over the head pin, squeezing it closed tightly over the beads using round-nose pliers. Cut off the excess pin and bend the remainder into a small loop. Attach the lobster clasp to one end and the chain link to the other end.

2

3 – To make the fringe, wrap a nylon thread filled with the semiprecious stones around the mass of beaded strands at the center of the necklace. Join the strands and then thread more semiprecious stones onto the thread until you've attained the desired length. Close off the end of the strand with a crimp bead. Continue this same work with other strands of nylon thread to create a cascade of fringe in the center of the necklace.

3

Sophistication
with flair

Materials
- 3 strands of Biwa pearls in the desired color
- 3 or 4 strands of colored beads in various sizes
- 2 crocheted bases (see step 1)
- nylon sewing thread
- harmonized lead wire
- beading needles
- crimp beads
- flat-nose or chain-nose pliers
- crochet hook
- thick cotton thread

1 – Use a crochet hook and thick cotton thread to crochet 2 firm round bases, as shown in the photograph. With a beading needle and nylon thread, sew the Biwa pearls around the edge of one crocheted base, attaching them closely beside one another and securing them tightly.

1

2 – Continue making a second and third ring of the pearls, in a fish-scale pattern, to complete the centerpiece. At the very center, attach a few pearls that are flat-nose or unusual in shape.

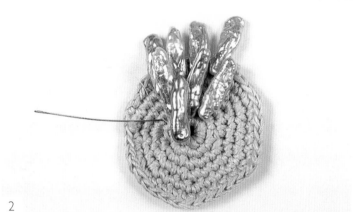

2

3 – After you have finished the center work, begin to attach the strands of pearls to the center using the lead wire. The first strands of beads should be relatively shorter than the others so that the necklace hangs properly and lies flat when worn.

3

4 – After you've finished attaching the side strands, sew the second crocheted base to the back of the embellished base.
At the end of each strand of pearls, attach a crimp bead. Squeeze each crimp bead firmly on the corresponding strand.

On the opposite page – Close-up of the back of the finished centerpiece and a photo of the necklace in all its beauty.

4

Beading and crocheting

Materials
- crocket hook
- thick cotton thread
- crocheted bases for bracelets and pendants
  (see step 1)
- scraps of chamois or suede
- beads
- semiprecious stones
- Swarovski crystals of your choice
- small cords
- sewing needle and thread
- Velcro hook-and-loop fastener
  (for bracelet closure)

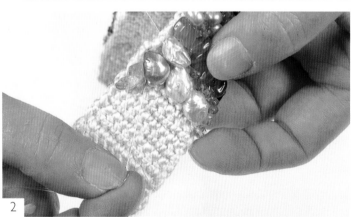

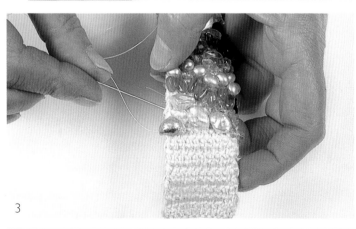

1 – For the base, crochet a firm rectangle (for a bracelet) or circle (for a pendant), or cut these shapes from scraps of chamois or suede.

2 – Sew the Velcro hook-and-loop tape to either side of the bracelet base, to make the closure. Begin to apply colored beads, sewing them to the base in a pleasing pattern.

3 – Continue embellishing the length of the bracelet, varying the pattern and beads in any way you wish. If you want to follow a particular or complex pattern, it helps to sketch or trace it on the base before you sew.

On the opposite page – Pendant embellished with semiprecious stones, Swarovski crystals, beads, and coral, all sewn on a special crocheted base. To wear the pendant as a necklace, insert a length of narrow cord through an embellished loop, which can be attached to the base of the pendant.

Below – Example of a bracelet sewn on a crocheted base. It is primarily coral, but includes beads and semiprecious stones.

Filigree necklace

Materials
- **filigree base, in gold or antique gold**
- **1 strand of citrine quartz pieces**
- **1 strand of amethyst pieces**
- **jewelry wire, 26-gauge**
- **wire cutters**

1 – The filigree base will serve as a support for the necklace pendant.

2 – Cut a piece of wire about 16". Bring the wire through a center hole on the base edge; affix with crimp bead, leaving short length of wire on the back. On the front, thread on amethyst pieces to cover one arc of the base, then bring the wire back through to the other side.

3 – Bring wire back through, tightly, and make a second arc parallel to the first; continue back and forth until the entire petal is covered. Twist the wire strands together at the back and cut off excess. Repeat until you have covered all petals on the base.

4 – For the centermost part, insert another thread and bring it through the center of the base, leaving a short "tail" in the back. Thread pieces of citrine quartz on the front and create a small arc. Bring the thread back through and reenter through the center holes of the base until entire piece is covered. Twist together all wire strands on back of pendant and cut excess. To attach pendant to necklace, make a small loop with a new wire and join it to an outer edge of pendant.

Below – Granite and citrine pendant, made with the same technique.

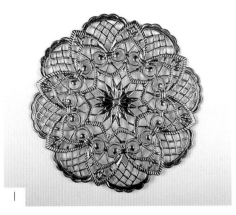

1

2

3

4

Crystal-spray ring

Materials
- **22 round crystals, Ø 5mm**
- **32 Swarovski crystals, octagonal, Ø 5 mm**
- **1 packet of colored beads**
- **nylon thread**
- **silver wire, 22-gauge**
- **ring bases**
- **round-nose pliers**
- **wire cutters**

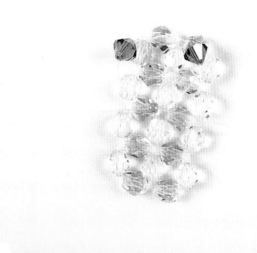

1

1 – Using the interweaving or "little boxes" technique (page 18) and the round crystals, make a rectangle 4 × 2 crystals in dimension for the base of the ring. Close off the threads with a double knot. Now you can begin the real work in creating this ring. Pass a new thread through the first crystal on the long side, insert 1 Swarovski crystal on one of two strands, and 1 bead and 1 crystal on the other strand. Then cross the thread with the single crystal through the bead.

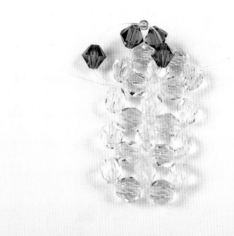

2

2 – Insert 1 crystal on each strand. Bring the strands below the base and twist together to tightly secure them. Continue this work until you've covered the base of the ring. At the end, secure the strands with a double knot and push them back through the first crystal before cutting the excess.

3 – With the silver wire and the ring base, make the support. Curl the excess wire into a loop or spiral for decoration.

3

Flowered ring and bracelet

Materials
For the ring
- 34/35 Swarovski crystals, Ø 5 mm
- 1 perforated disk
- ring base
- nylon thread
- crimp beads
- flat-nose or chain-nose pliers

Materials
For the bracelet
- about 50 crystals, Ø 5 mm
- 1 perforated disk
- 1 bracelet base
- nylon thread
- crimp beads
- flat-nose or chain-nose pliers

1 – Cut a piece of nylon thread and place a crimp bead on one end. Pass the other end through the center of the perforated disk, back to front. Thread on a crystal and a bead; pass the thread back through the same crystal, flipping the bead so it lies flat, and pull tight. Pull the thread back through to the underside of the perforated disk.

1

2 – Bring the thread up again and continue until you have covered the entire perforated disk. Close off the thread with a crimp bead.

2

3 – Position the perforated disk on the ring base and pinch the 4 support staples until secure.

   If you wish to make a bracelet, follow the same steps but use the bracelet support.

3

Sea-urchin ring

Materials
- about 105 crystals, Ø 5 mm
- 1 packet of colored beads
  (in the same shade as the
  crystals)
- 1 perforated disk
- ring base
- crimp beads
- nylon thread
- flat-nose or chain-nose
  pliers

1 – Cut a piece of nylon thread and place a crimp bead on one end. Push the other end through the center of the perforated disk. Thread on 1 crystal, 6 beads, 1 crystal, 6 beads (or more, as shown in photo), 1 crystal, 1 bead. Pass the thread back through the nearest crystal, flipping the single bead so it lies flat. Continue pushing the thread down through the other beads and crystals, emerging on the back of the disk.

1

2 – Bring the thread up again and continue until you have covered the entire perforated disk.

2

3 – To complete your work, bring the thread to the back of the disk and close it off with a crimp bead. Position the perforated disk on the ring base and pinch the 4 support staples until secure.

3

Beaded ring

Materials
- 14/15 glazed glass beads in various colors
- 1 larger, colored glass bead
- silver wire, 22-gauge
- ring mandrel
- wire cutters
- round-nose pliers

1 – Cut a 60" length of silver wire. Thread on your choice of beads. Leaving about 4" of wire free on both ends, loop the wire around the each individual bead. Make sure to leave a bit of space between them.

2 – Wrap a free wire end (what's left after you have threaded the beads together) around the ring ruler at the desired size. Leave a small piece free at the end; wrap it around the rest of the wire to secure it. At the other side of this piece, thread on the largest glass bead; it will sit atop the mass of beads, standing out from the others.

3 – Wrap beaded wire around central glass bead in concentric circles for desired form. With the remaining wire (4"), make a loop around the base to secure the support of the rest of your work.

1

2

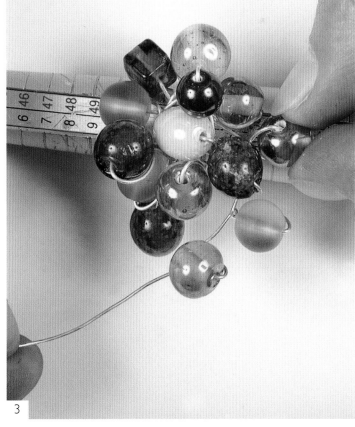

3

Swarovski earrings

Materials
- **86 Swarovski crystals**
- **nylon thread**
- **earring hooks**
- **crimp beads**

1 – Insert 5 crystals on a nylon thread about 24" in length.

2 – Cross the strands through the last crystal and pull tightly, bringing your work to the center.

3 – Then, insert 3 crystals on 1 thread, and 1 crystal on the other.

4 – Cross the strand with 3 crystals through the single crystal.

5 – On the strand that you just pushed through the single crystal, insert another crystal. On the other strand, thread on 2 crystals. Cross this thread, carrying 2 crystals, through the single crystal.

6 – Continue until you've finished the cluster. You can mount one or two silver elements on the center of the earring (above) or cover the rest of the thread with the same crystals, securing them at the end with a crimp bead (shown on page 130).

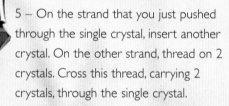

1

2

3

4

5

6

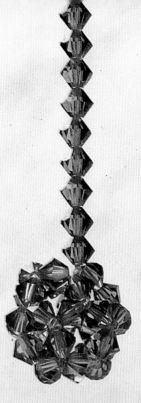

Silver earrings

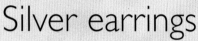

Materials
- 1 small piece of silver chain link
- 12 assorted silver bobbles (4 of each kind)
- 4 sapphire beads
- 2 earring hooks
- silver wire
- head pins
- eye pins
- round-nose pliers
- wire cutters

1 – From the silver chain link, cut 2 pieces 4" long and 2 pieces 1" to 1 1/4" long. Using a head pin, attach an earring hook to the middle link of one 4" chain. Using an eye hook, attach a sapphire bead to the middle link of the other 4" chain. Attach a silver bobble to one end of each 1" to 1 1/4" chain. For the centerpiece, thread 2 silver bobbles, 1 sapphire bead, and 2 silver bobbles on silver wire in a symmetrical arrangement.

2 – Using round-nose pliers, bend each end of the silver wire into a ring. Attach one end of each chain to one ring. Repeat on the other side, to form the pendant earring with dangling sapphire bead and silver bobbles.

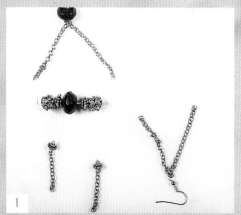

1

2

3 – Use the flat-nose or chain-nose pliers to open and close the loops when joining the components together.

3

Mosaic necklace

Materials
- semiprecious
  stones in various
  shapes and sizes,
  in the desired
  quantity
- pearls
- Biwa pearls
- silver wire, 22- and
  20-gauge
- 1 3/4 yards colored
  organza ribbon
- round-nose pliers
- wire cutters

1 – Cut a piece of 20-gauge silver wire and insert it through the predrilled hole in a stone. With the round-nose pliers, make a loop at the base of the stone. Wrap the remaining wire around the stone, making rings and loops until you are pleased with its appearance.

2 – With the same wire, make the hook. Do this by making a ring around the base of the round-nose pliers, starting at the tip and wrapping the wire around in a disk shape. Make sure to keep your work flat, and continue until you've run out of wire.

3 – Follow steps 1 and 2 for all of the stones. Wire-wrapped (or "caged") stones are presented here.

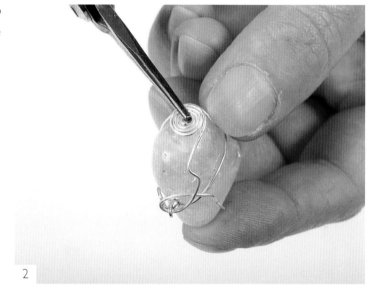

4 – Thread the 22-gauge silver wire through the hooks at the top of each stone to tie the stones together. Wrap and join the stones, constructing a design that's to your liking. Piece by piece, add stones of various shapes and colors.

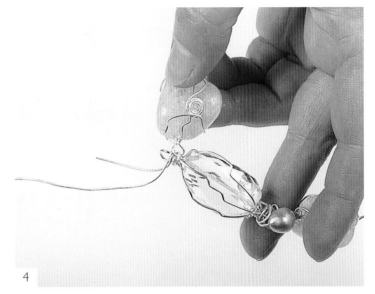

4

5 – To finish your composition, cover the space between each of the semiprecious stones with the pearls in a way that embellishes your work.

5

6 – Organza ribbon can be attached to the finished centerpiece, shown here, to make a necklace.

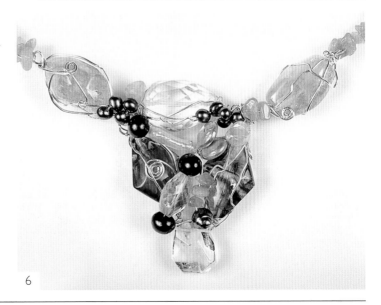

6

Vienna beads

Materials

For the earrings
- glass beads, square and round
- iridescent beads in black, ruby, and pink
- crystals in a color of your choice
- sewing thread
- lead wire
- crimp beads
- 2 earring hooks
- beading needle

For the necklace
- glass beads, square and round
- cork bead for the centerpiece
- iridescent beads, 2 packets each of black, ruby, and pink
- colored crystals
- sewing thread
- lead wire
- spring clip
- jump ring
- beading needle

1 – This type of work involves covering large glass beads with smaller beads and crystals. Double up the sewing thread, make a knot at one end, and then pass the thread through the hole of a large bead so that the knot stays at the base. On the doubled thread, insert as many small beads as you need to cover the length of the glass bead; secure the end with a small knot.

2 – Bring the needle back through the inside of the large bead. Make another knot at the end, and insert more beads on the remaining thread. Continue in this way until you've covered the entire bead. Securely tie the thread at the base and cut off the excess.

3 – To make earrings, insert the following items, in order, on the lead wire: 1 crimp bead, 1 crystal, 1 gold ball, 1 crystal, 1 covered glass bead, and 1 crystal. Block off the end by making a small ring around the base of the earring hook, which will attach the pieces together.

To make a necklace, use as many covered beads as are necessary to obtain a necklace of the length you desire. Insert a jump ring on one end and a spring clip on the other.

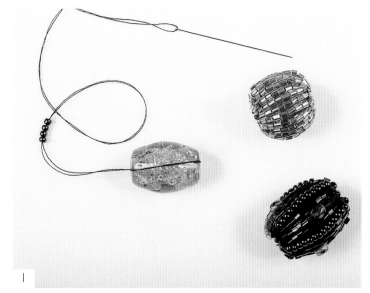

Silk and glass

Materials
- 13 1/8 yards of braided silk thread and cord in various colors
- Venetian glass centerpiece
- 6 black glass beads
- 2 bead covers
- 2 head pins
- lobster clasp

1 – Cut the braided thread into 12 strands, each 40" in length. Gather the strands together, fold them in half, and tie a single knot at the center. Thread on the Venetian glass centerpiece, pushing it all the way to the knot, and then tie another knot to tightly secure the centerpiece.

2 – Insert a glass bead on various threads, and position it beside one of the two knots made in step 1.

3 – Make another knot on the other side of the bead you've just added. Continue by adding on 2 more glass beads, alternating them with knots. Mirror your work on one side with the other, so that the necklace is even. Bring all the threads together and cut off any excess to even out the length. At each end, tie the strands at the base with a small length of wire. Place a bead cover over the wire-bound thread and press it firmly with pliers until secure. Then, on each side, affix the clasp elements.

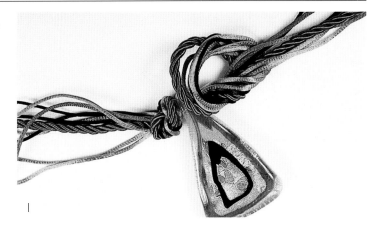

More silk

With the same technique as described on page 139, you can make a multistrand necklace in black silk, adorned with beads, crystals, or other pieces.

1 – Take 70 pieces of silk thread, each 40" in length, and level the ends. Separate out 6 strands from the mass and put them aside. Make a loose knot in the center of the 64 strands. Fold the reserved 6 strands in half, to make a 20" length, and push them through the center of the knot for the fringe. Finally, pull the knot tight.

1

2 – Thread a glass bead on the fringe, which is made with 20" pieces of thread. To make this easier, separate the threads into smaller bundles and wrap adhesive tape around the ends to push them through.

2

3 – At the base of the glass bead, make a neat knot, keeping all the stands together.

3

4 – On one side of the center knot (which you made in step 1) insert a glass piece and, with all the strands, make another large knot. Then, insert a second glass bead and follow it with another knot. Mirror your work on the other side of the center knot.

5 – To close off the necklace, bring the 2 masses of thread together and tie them with a decorative knot. Level the ends of the threads to form a nice tassel.

Below – The finished necklace. A very refined accessory that can be worn with long, loose clothing in daytime or evening.

Stringed beads

Materials
- 8 lengths, 40" each, of waxed thread in gold, 1.6 mm
- 3 crystal wheels or large beads
- various Venetian glass beads in amber color
- flowered beads
- crystals in various sizes and colors
- antique burned gold pearls
- silver baroque pearls

1 – Double over the 8 strands of waxed thread and make a knot 3/4" from the center to close it off. Using the locked loop technique (page 25), make several knots around the loop with a single strand.

2 – Insert 1 crystal on the single strand, secure it with a knot, and then cut off the excess thread. On each of the remaining 15 strands, thread on a single bead and push it up toward the locked loop. Choose different types of beads in complementary colors.

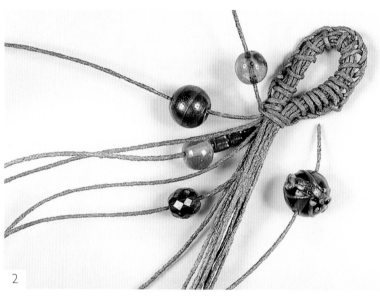

3 – Make another knot about 3" from the base of the locked loop, using all of the strands.

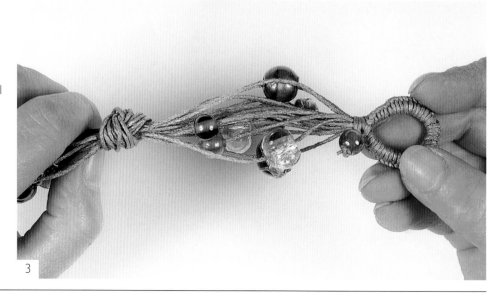

4 – On strands below knot, insert more crystals, beads, and pearls. Secure with a knot, using all threads, about 2 1/2" from previous knot. Continue steps until you're at halfway point (center of necklace).

4

5 – Insert beads and pearls on each strand, divide into 3 groups, and knot off. Insert a crystal wheel on each. Tie off each with a knot, but leave room between knots, so the crystals can move. Add more beads below each knot and, at 5" from the knot, make another knot using all strands.

5

6 – Finish center part, working symmetrically on each side. After last knot, thread a crystal on each, of 3 strands making a knot with all strands. Insert flowered bead on end of 1 strand, to use as a clasp, securing it with a knot at base. Cut off excess thread.

6

For summer

Materials
For the necklace
- 6 pieces of linen thread, 2 3/4 yards each
- blue-colored crystals
- 1 large crystal for the clasp
- fabric flowers
- wool needle

For the bracelet
- 7 pieces of thread, each 40"
- assorted colored crystals

BLUE FLOWERED NECKLACE

1 – Fold the 6 pieces of thread in half and make a locked loop (page 25) at one end, securing all the strands at the base with a large knot.

1

2 – Continue by inserting crystals of various colors and shapes on the 6 strands. Then, 2" from the first knot, make a second loose knot.

2

3 – On one of the strands, with the help of the needle, insert 1 fabric flower and 1 crystal. On each of 2 other strands, insert 1 crystal. Make another loose knot with all 6 strands.

3

4 – Repeat the above steps a second time using the same strands, and make another knot. On the loose end of the strands, thread on various crystals and block them off with a knot. Continue following these steps until you've reached the desired length. At the end, insert 1 large crystal (which, when pushed through the locked loop, works as a clasp), and tie off both ends with a knot. Level the strands on either side.

4

5 – To complete the necklace, make a series of small tassels. Cut a few pieces of thread in various lengths and tie them to the strands at the end of the necklace.

5

6 – On the end of each tassel, attach a crystal and make a knot. Cut off the excess thread.

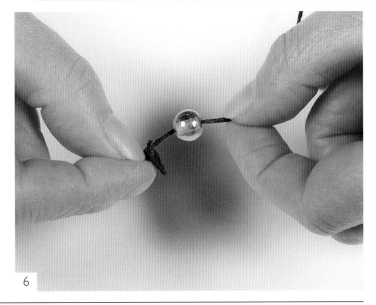

6

BRACELET IN NATURAL THREAD

1 – Fold 7 strands in half so that you're working with 14 pieces, each 40" in length. Make a locked loop (page 25) at the folded end. Below the locked loop, make a loose knot using all the threads.

2 – Begin by alternating between loops and knots. To do this, take the bundle of thread and tie it around itself, creating a loop, which you'll then secure with a loose knot. Continue doing this in a pattern that's to your liking.

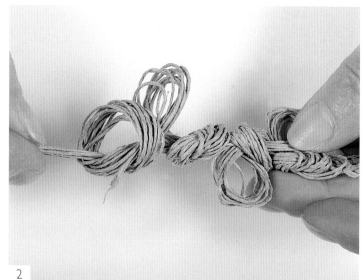

3 – Terminate the sequence of loops and knots by threading 1 crystal on the strands, which will act as part of a clasp. Cut a few lengths of thread and tie them to the base of the knots to make tassels.

4 – At the bottom of these strands insert a few crystals, which you'll block off with small knots. You can use crystals of various colors and sizes.

5 – Once you're finished adding the crystals, cut the excess thread below the knots.

6 – The technique for this bracelet, and the grouping of crystals, is intended to give your bracelet a unique look.

Rustic elegance

Materials
- 76 yards linen thread
- 1 large gold bead
- 6 Syrian glass beads
- gold beads
- head pins
- thread covers
- jump ring
- lobster clasp

1 – Cut 64 pieces of thread, each 40" in length. Thread the large gold ball onto the strands, and bring it to the center. Using all of the strands, make a knot on both sides of the bead. On either side, divide the strands into 2 bunches, and then thread on 2 beads facing each other, 1 on each bunch. Then make another knot with all the strands. Cut 8 pieces of thread, each 20" in length. Tie them in a knot between the two glass beads, leaving one side of the remaining thread a bit longer than the other.

2 – On the shorter side, insert a glass bead and block it off with a knot. Cut off the excess thread evenly.

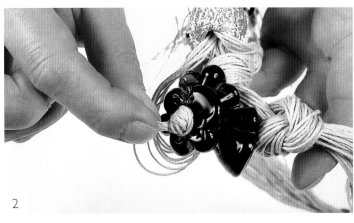

3 – Run the longer side through the center of the large gold bead, and make a knot about 2 1/2" away from the bead. On the open thread, insert glass beads, distancing them by making small knots between them to create a cascade. Cut off the excess thread. Repeat this on the other side of the necklace. Tie each end of the necklace tightly. Push a head pin through each end, and position the thread cover over it. Then squeeze the thread cover tightly until secure. Attach a jump ring on one side and a lobster clasp on the other.

Jewelry of the sea

Materials
For the necklace
- 5 large cork balls, Ø 18 mm
- 10 pieces of bamboo coral
- 15 small cork balls, Ø 12 mm
- 30 turquoise-colored crystals
- eye pins

For the earrings
- 8 turquoise-colored crystals
- 2 large cork balls, Ø 18 mm
- 2 small cork balls, Ø 12 mm
- 2 pieces of bamboo coral
- 4 eye pins
- 2 head pins
- 2 earring hooks

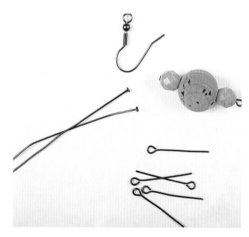

For the earrings, push a head pin through 1 crystal, 1 small cork ball, and 1 crystal; cut off the excess and make a small ring at the end. Insert an eye pin through a piece of bamboo coral; cut off the excess and make a small ring, attaching it to the cork ball piece before closing off. Insert on an eye pin 1 crystal, 1 large cork ball, and 1 crystal. Join with a small ring to the coral piece. Affix the earring hook to the eye hook loop. Make a second earring to match.

Use the same technique to make a matching necklace or the Bamboo cane and coral set shown to the right.

Marine-style necklace, with black linen tassels, shells, and turquoise-colored crystals.

Index